THE CRASH OF

LITTLE EVA

BARRY RALPH

PELICAN PUBLISHING COMPANY
Gretna 2006

First published as *Savage Wilderness:*
   The Epic Outback Search for the Crew of Little
   Eva by University of Queensland Press, 2004
Published by arrangement with the author by
   Pelican Publishing Company, Inc., 2006

LCN: 940.544973
ISBN-13: 978-1-58980-447-0

Printed in the United States of America

Published by Pelican Publishing Company, Inc.
1000 Burmaster Street, Gretna, Louisiana 70053

THE CRASH OF
LITTLE EVA

Contents

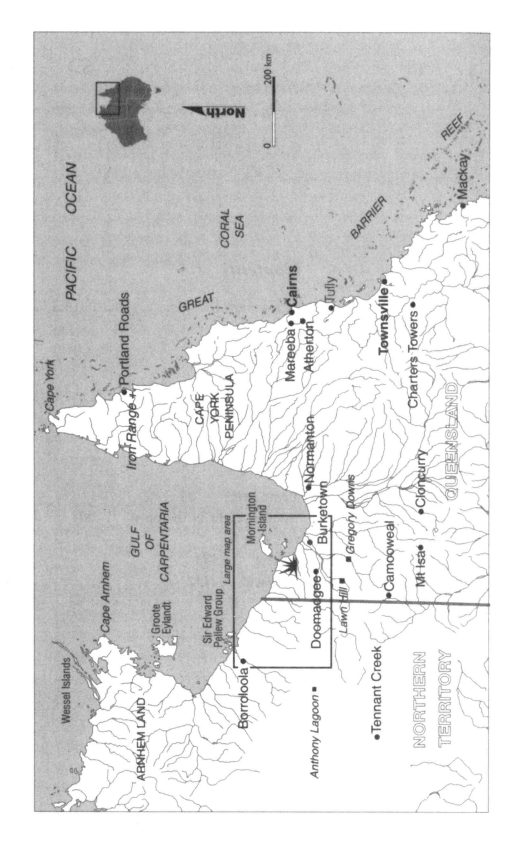

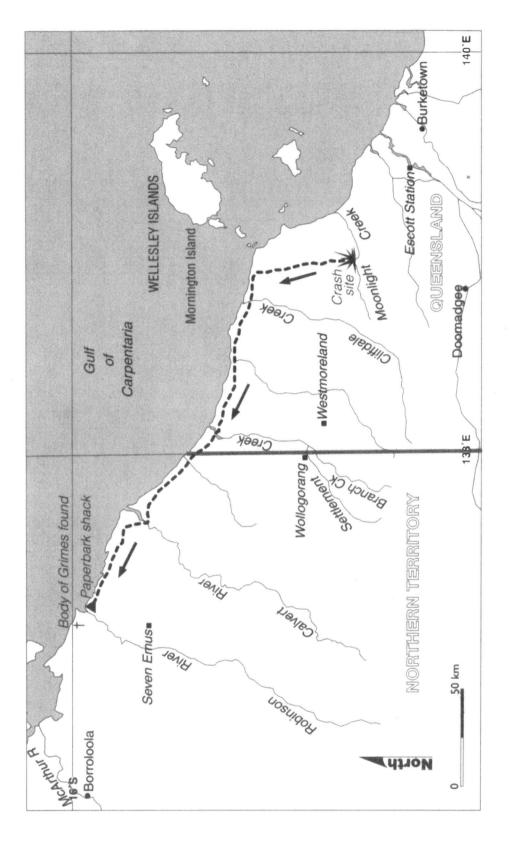

Preface

My original inspiration to write a book about *Little Eva* was the compelling nature of this story. Yet despite the existence of numerous articles and a television documentary, there were no fully documented accounts of this dramatic episode.

During research for my book *They Passed This Way* I came across the police files relating to the original ground search. As I examined the yellowing papers in the Queensland State Archives, my enthusiasm for this project was ignited.

There were literally hundreds of archival documents and dozens of reports relating to every aspect of the police search. Although armed forces personnel, civilians and Indigenous people were all involved, this was a police search and they were responsible for meticulously compiling, storing and preserving these reports.

Over the years many people have claimed involvement with the original searches, with some even claiming to have found the aircraft prior to the official search party.

The evidence suggests otherwise. Written within hours or days of the events, the archived reports convey in minute detail the unfolding story of the *Little Eva* drama and its aftermath. *The Crash of Little Eva* is based on these definitive historical documents.

The B-24D Liberator that crashed near Moonlight Creek in December 1942 came from the 321st Squadron of the 90th Bomb Group and I was fortunate to make contact with several members of the 90th Bomb Group veterans organisation.

I was delighted by the response I received from my American colleagues.

Wiley Woods Jr is the official historian for the 90th Bomb Group and I owe him a considerable debt for allowing me access to his previous accounts of the group. He also answered many questions about those brave airmen of long ago.

Thomas Fetter, Loyde Adams and the late James McMurria all offered expert advice and invaluable recollections. I cannot hope to repay the debt that I owe Walter Higgins of San Antonio, Texas. Walter was a former pilot of the 321st Squadron and knew all those involved in this story.

Much of this book could not have been written without the support and patience of this remarkable man who, at 89, is wondering what to do when he eventually reaches old age.

I would also like to convey my appreciation to the family of the ill-fated 2nd Lieutenant Arthur Speltz. It was Mark Speltz who offered to make available his late uncle's papers and letters: a large collection of photographs, newspaper cuttings and numerous documents relating to the *Little Eva* tragedy. Through these family artefacts I gained a better understanding of Arthur 'Tony' Speltz, and one that went well beyond the superficiality of name, rank and serial number.

A similar debt is owed to Mrs Arvilla 'Billie' Wilson, the widow of the late Loy Wilson, who was one of the six men to survive the crash in the early morning hours of 2 December 1942. Mrs Wilson supplied much lucid detail and provided access to many of her husband's papers, clippings and reports as well as several rare photographs. I also made contact with the family of the late Norman Crosson, *Little Eva*'s pilot. His son, John Crosson of Andersonville, South Carolina, answered many questions about his esteemed father who enjoyed a long and distinguished career in the United States Air Force.

Unfortunately, the remarkable Grady Gaston died shortly before I began work on this project, however his widow answered a detailed questionnaire for me. Mrs Gaston clarified many unanswered questions and also made available her late husband's mementos from the incident including letters, photographs and copies of scripts from radio programs in which Grady had participated.

Members of the Queensland Police Force were also supportive of my research. Police Commissioner Bob Atkinson took a personal interest in the project and I took full advantage of available police resources including the Queensland Police Museum.

Duncan Leask and Lisa Jones supplied the service records of those involved in the search and even located century-old design plans of the outback police buildings.

John Cummins helped me locate former policemen who had long since left the force. Former assistant-police commissioner Vern McDonald is the oldest surviving senior police veteran and a virtual encyclopedia of the force's history. He effortlessly recalled details of this incident and valuable insights into the police involved. I owe him a great deal for his patience and interest.

Senior Sergeant Stephen Stafford and Senior Constable Michael 'Moose' Musumeci of Doomadgee Police Station organised an Anzac Day commemoration for the personnel of *Little Eva*, which included the unveiling of a plaque in the town centre, listing the names of the crew. It was a privilege to attend this event and to enjoy the hospitality of police, locals and Aboriginal elders. Moose also arranged an emotional visit to the wreck site. The Doomadgee elders were invaluable in providing information and insights on the Indigenous people involved in the search for survivors: thanks to Ada Walden, Clara Foster, Eva and June Gilbert and Flora Nero. I also owe a debt of gratitude to Patrick 'Monkey' Jack — the main catalyst for a rare performance of the Aeroplane Dance, which was major highlight of the Doomadgee visit.

A special vote of thanks to John Keighran who spoke for hours about his late father, Jack. Pat Hagarty was no less forthcoming when we spoke about his remarkable father, Bob. Pat also supplied several priceless photographs.

Writer and historian Jim Eames was also an indispensable information source. Jim had earlier spoken to many of the *Little Eva* protagonists when conducting research for his excellent book *The Searchers* and generously allowed me access to all of his notes and papers relating to the episode.

Bill Bentson, an expatriate American veteran, is the ultimate source for all things military during the war years and his co-operation is most appreciated. I would also like to thank Peter Dunn, Col Benson, Rupert Goodman, Bob Pieper, Bob Alford, Roger Marks, David Vincent, Ken Lee, Mike Longton, Cec Parsons, Doug and Fay Jones, Neville and Lynn Meyers and the late Sid Bromley as well as the staff of the John Oxley Library, the Queensland State Archives, the Australian National Archives and the Northern Territory Archives who allowed me access to their collections and resources.

Finally I would like to thank my family for their ongoing support and for their understanding in regard to my passion for the future of the past.

THE CRASH OF
LITTLE EVA

CHAPTER ONE

'I certainly feel good about enlisting'

World War II was a conflict on a massive scale but not all of the protagonists were military forces. Frequently the forces of nature proved to be an equally formidable enemy. In December 1942, the natural environment became a hostile opponent for the American crew of the B-24 bomber, *Little Eva*. During the bitter turmoil of the war against Japan in the Pacific, a savage wilderness became their unexpected foe.

The young men who found themselves in this terrifying predicament came from different cities, different professions and different backgrounds. The only common denominator was their youth. No amount of training or material support could prepare these airmen for the experience that lay in wait for them. Social standing, wealth and rank became irrelevant during their long ordeal and the man thought the least likely to succeed became the most likely to survive.

The journey that led them to their destiny in the Australian outback began with the events of a bright Sunday morning in Hawaii in December 1941.

The birth of the 90th Bombardment Group in early 1942 was a direct result of the death of the American Pacific Fleet at Pearl Harbor. The 'Day of Infamy' had belatedly thrust the United States of

America into a global war. President Franklin D. Roosevelt immediately called the nation to arms and began the greatest mobilisation in the nation's history. For decades the United States had enjoyed the peaceful bliss of isolationism. Germany's military aggression in Europe had alarmed the politicians and the populace of America, but it had not lessened the resolve of the people to remain neutral and not become involved in another European conflict. Since the early days of the European war, President Roosevelt had been supporting Britain with essential supplies, which meant that the country was engaging in a kind of clandestine war with Germany.

As late as November 1941 Roosevelt was still advocating neutrality. He knew the mood well: only 8 per cent of the US population were interventionists; the remainder wanted nothing to do with a foreign war.

Japan's military expansion was being stalled by the Allied oil and raw-material embargo and the freezing of all Japan's assets in America. However, Japan remained defiant and began to focus on strategic objectives. In order to continue armed aggression in the Far East, access to the oil-rich Netherlands East Indies and Malaya was essential. The only deterrent to the Japanese plans was the American fleet based in Hawaii and to a lesser extent the British naval base at Singapore.

It was from carrier-based aircraft that the Japanese attacked the American Pacific Fleet at Pearl Harbor. In less than three hours, eight capital ships were sunk or severely damaged, 166 aircraft were destroyed — mostly on the ground — and 2403 Americans died. It was the end of America's isolationism and the beginning of global war. After twenty-three years of peace, Uncle Sam was once again embroiled in another war.

The 1930s depression, America's aloofness and its indifference to national defence had made the great Arsenal of Democracy a third-rate military power. The armed forces were undermanned, with meagre equipment that was mostly antiquated and obsolete.

All was not lost. The Selective Service Act, a Roosevelt initiative that led to the first ever peacetime draft, had put a million men in uniform and in training. The National Guard was also mobilised, and a week after the 'Day of Infamy' sixteen million men had rushed to the nation's draft boards.

America's greatest weapons were its mobilisation and its production capacity. Japan's mistake was in underestimating the resolve of the United States. From the early days of the conflict, it was obvious that there would be no appeasement and no negotiated peace treaties in a prolonged conflict. However, full mobilisation and major offensive strategies would take time — at least a year.

The United States Army's aviation group from 1926 to 1941 was called the Army Air Corps. During the 1930s the Roosevelt Administration was mostly indifferent to the needs of the Air Corps. Indeed, until the 1920s the government had been indifferent to the value of *any* aircraft. Traditional bureaucrats believed that aircraft were 'simply a means of conveyance, captained by chauffeurs'. It was not until a young major called Henry 'Hap' (short for Happy) Arnold began to advocate air power as a potent weapon that the situation would change. Arnold was an experienced flyer, having been in aviation since its beginning. He was personally instructed by one of the Wright Brothers and received his wings in 1911. In 1921, in a single-seat aircraft, Arnold raced a group of carrier pigeons from Portland to San Francisco. The stunt was a direct result of a challenge by a national newspaper. Arnold beat the pigeons by forty-one hours. It was in no sense a match-up, but it created valuable publicity for the cause. The United States government was an interested observer. Four years later, a pugnacious Brigadier General, Billy Mitchell, bombed two obsolete American battleships from an aircraft off the Atlantic Coast. This time the government did take notice. Mitchell was promptly court-martialled and he ultimately resigned from the Air Corps, but he had made his point and his views on the benefits of strategic bombing would prove prophetic.

The Corps were convinced that the country required heavy

bombers to aid the nation's defence. However, most military experts disagreed. They believed that the main function of the Air Corps would be to assist the navy in coastal defence and the army in ground manoeuvres. In 1934 a special fact-finding group within the War Department concluded that 'independent air missions will have little effect upon the issue of battle and none upon the outcome of the war'.

With the economic depression of the 1930s and diminishing federal revenues, the plight of the Air Corps became a low priority and progress was slow. In 1934, the service managed to win approval to order its first fleet of heavy bombers and Boeing began production on the B-17. By 1939, thirteen had been delivered, with forty more on order. The war in Europe changed everything. Charles Lindbergh, trans-Atlantic pathfinder and national hero, had returned from Europe and was profoundly impressed by the Luftwaffe. 'They are more formidable than all the other European nations put together,' he told Arnold. 'The only weapon that they don't have is a heavy bomber as good as the B-17 Flying Fortress.' Lindbergh soon found himself on a blue-ribbon panel headed by Brigadier General W. G. Kilner to discuss the needs of air defence. The conclusion was a total reverse of previous strategic thinking. The United States could no longer rely solely on naval and coastal artillery defences to repel a potential invader. The Kilner board recommended 'new long-range aircraft that are capable of attacking enemy bases'.

The European war created a demand for more equipment and an independent air force. The fall of France in June 1940 attested to the might of the Luftwaffe. The value of air power was no longer in doubt. When Arnold, now chief of the Air Corps, went to Capitol Hill to discuss appropriations he was told that any amount would be granted. 'All you have to do is ask for it,' said Senator Henry Cabot Lodge.

The United States entered the Pacific War with 25 000 personnel and 4000 aircraft. These figures would dramatically increase as the Air Corps took advantage of the blank cheque and Uncle Sam's production potential. The new arrivals of men and machines resulted in the Army Air Corps and the Air Force Combat Command being amalgamated under the control of Arnold. On 20 June 1941 the two groups became the United States Army Air Forces (USAAF). This new group still operated under the auspices of the Army group, but it had considerable freedom, with Arnold reporting directly to the Chiefs of Staff.

The 90th Bombardment Group was a genuine 'war baby', conceived out of the legacy of the Pearl Harbor disaster. The fledgling group was activated at Key Field, Meridian, Mississippi, on 15 April 1942. It was something less than a formidable force. There were no planes, no pilots and little equipment. The seventy-three enlisted men spent their time doing drill manoeuvres and awaiting events. On 15 May the group moved to Barksdale Field, Louisiana, which was a more comfortable billet. There was a swimming pool, a gymnasium, tennis courts and a friendly town called Shreveport nearby. The war seemed a long way away.

By the end of the month the organisation began to grow. Men and machines arrived and training began in earnest. The group consisted of men who were professional officers and those who were drafted, most as a result of the Selective Services Act. The criteria for officer entry into the USAAF were demanding. Walter Higgins was an ambitious young man from Fort Worth, Texas, who graduated with 115 other young men from Brooks Field, San Antonio, on 9 January 1942. It was a memorable day. In addition to being commissioned, Higgins received his wings in the morning and was married in the afternoon. He described the requirements to get into the Air Corps:

At least two years of college or equivalent was required. There were a lot of applicants turned down because of the strict physical examination. Eyes, heart, coordination were all monitored. Even after one made the grade for flight training things got tougher. There wasn't a lot of time to teach you. You either did it right or you were on your way to other things. About half of your class would not make the grade. In my class about half failed Primary Flight School and many more Basic Flight School. In Advanced Flight School the only ones that failed to get their wings were those who managed to kill themselves flying. There were many training accidents. Most of us were not career officers. We joined because we were aware of the threat of war. Several of us in college quit and joined the Air Corps. I don't recall knowing any pilots that were drafted. By and large most of the personnel in the Air Corps, officers and enlisted men, were volunteers.

Higgins was twenty-five when he received his wings. His fellow graduates came from all over America: James A. McMurria was from South Carolina, Lyle Schoenauer from Nebraska, George W. Sellmer from Illinois, Norman R. Crosson from Ohio, Edwin Holloway from New Jersey, Donald Elder from New York and Arthur Speltz from Minnesota. Speltz's letters to his family convey his buoyant enthusiasm:

Well I certainly feel good about enlisting. We are certain to get service in the Air Corps. Plenty of hard work and not much time to study. When I sit and listen to our professor's lectures, I certainly learn something. Also get a lot of flying instructions. I soloed on February 6 — just a start. Should get my dress uniform soon and a short haircut.

All were young and eager and they were soon dispersed into the ever-expanding USAAF. Pilots were allocated to fighters, light and heavy bombers, observation units and other specialties. Second lieutenants were dispatched in twos or threes into various combat units.

'Planes, we need more planes,' General Arnold told President Roosevelt. 'We need 50 000 new planes in 1942.' Roosevelt responded, 'No, we'll build 60 000 this year and 125 000 in 1943.' In fact, the United States built 47 836 planes in 1942 and 85 898 in 1943. The USAAF took delivery of 295 000 aircraft during the war, 19 203 of which were the B-24 Consolidated Liberator.

During the 1930s, military analysts had stressed the need for heavy bombers to protect the American coastline from invasion. The B-24 was developed by Consolidated Aircraft in response to a request from the Air Corps to create a bomber that would be superior to the B-17 especially in range, bomb capacity and altitude. Drawing heavily on the Boeing Company's B-15s and B-17s, as well as the Consolidated P4Y flying boat, the first prototype, XB-24, flew for the first time on 29 December 1939.

It was an innovative machine, with turbo-supercharged engines — a Davis 'wet wing' arrangement with the fuel being stored evenly along the entire wing section. It also had considerable armour protection. However, it was an ugly brute, a fact that troubled Consolidated Aircraft President Reuben Fleet to the extent that he promptly ordered an extra three feet to be added to the snub nose to make it 'look prettier'. The Air Corps soon ordered 2434 Liberators to be delivered in 1942. Most of them were the B-24Ds, which were armed with .50 calibre machine guns, including two tail guns and two nose guns, as well as two located in the middle section, on either side of the fuselage, commonly called waist guns. The B-24Ds could carry up to 8000 pounds of bombs and fly at nearly 300 miles per hour at 30 000 feet. The aircraft had a range of 2800 miles and cost $336 000. Those who flew the B-24Ds knew that they could 'go anywhere and do anything'; better still, they were 'tough bastards'. Ultimately, many believed that the B-24D was the best aircraft Consolidated ever built.

Pearl Harbor gave Henry Arnold a third star. His decisiveness was matched by his influence. With thousands of aircraft being delivered, Arnold reshaped the AAF. Unlike the Air Corps, where most officers on the payroll were pilots, the AAF would need to find and train over 100 000 officers to be 'ground pounders'. Arnold insisted that

Consolidated and Boeing train five mechanics for every aircraft that came off the line. At one stage during the war, the personnel for the AAF exceeded two and a half million.

Arnold's favourite phrase was 'Keep 'em flying'. Before long he had the men and the machines to do so. The term became a catchcry for the nation. It was a rallying call for the defiant and a cheerful response to adversity. The day after Pearl Harbor, Glenn Miller and his orchestra recorded a piece called 'Keep 'em Flying' for RCA Victor in New York. Miller soon joined the AAF, as did other celebrities. The country had never seen such a devotion to national duty.

The men of the fledgling 90th Bomb Group wanted to do their share. When the brand new B-24Ds arrived at Barksdale, the men knew that they had the tools to do the job. The group began to structure its forces. Four squadrons were formed, the 319th, 320th, 321st and 400th. They were led by Major Arthur H. Rogers, Major Margraves, Captain Delbert Hahn and Captain Harry J. Bullis. The Group Commander was Lieutenant Colonel Eugene P. Mussett.

The group was soon on the move again. This time it was to a new base at Greenville, North Carolina. The town of Greenville was not the entertainment capital of the world and there was little to do during liberty time. One popular haunt for the men was a place called Shorty's Barbecue, on the corner of North Camp and Old Camp Roads. Jack and Eva Coyle bought the place in 1940, and the posting of the 90th Bomb Group to the area was a financial bonanza for them. It was standing room only. 'The boys were there all the time,' remembered Jack. 'The MPs were always circling around the place.'

Lieutenant Norman Crosson, a pilot in the 321st squadron, was a regular at Shorty's. The 26-year-old officer had grown up quickly. Born in Cincinnati, Ohio, he had felt the depression more than most his age. His father was a brick mason who had struggled for work during those dark days. Young Norm would leave home before daylight and shovel coal in those houses lucky enough to be able to afford the commodity. He would do the same in the evenings. During school hours he sold candy bars to make enough money for the family supper. He did anything and everything to help support his family, which included a sister called Mary and a younger, physically handicapped brother who Norman called Yonce.

The future looked bleak for Crosson until he answered an advertisement in a local newspaper. Uncle Sam was looking for young men to enroll in the Air Cadet School. Norm's decision to pursue a military career changed his life. His career peaked when he became a lieutenant in the Army Air Corp.

Crosson liked the barbeque and sandwiches at Shorty's. Like most of the guys he couldn't get enough of the jukebox. The beer was always cold — that is, if you could get near the bar. Eva Coyle, an enormous woman — Norm guessed around 300 pounds — was the enforcer in the establishment. She could take care of herself and then some. Crosson heard that she'd once thrown a man through a glass door. Jack taught Eva to ride a motorcycle and she became a local legend; everybody called her 'Little Eva'.

The 90th Bomb Group began a period of intense training, including a rigorous schedule of cross-country flying. On 7 July 1942, a B-24D on its way from Barksdale to Greenville crashed into a Georgia hilltop. Lieutenant Earl M. Hobson and his crew were killed. They became the first of the 820 men from the 90th Bomb Group who would die for their country.

Six weeks later, the group was on the move again. This time the posting was Ford's new Willow Run plant at Ypsilante, Michigan.

On August 14th, Lieutenant Eugene King and his crew of eight died when their B-24 crashed into a Michigan cornfield near Hastings.

The rumours that the group would soon be shipped out proved correct and in early September the group was on the move yet again. It was a foggy, dim and miserable night on September 3rd when 1300 men, mostly 'ground pounders', boarded the steamship S.S. *Republic*, an old tub that had taken their fathers to the war in Europe a generation before. As the old vessel slipped under the Golden Gate Bridge, the men were told that their destination was Hawaii.

The group's aircraft were to be flown direct to Hawaii. It was an ambitious and dangerous exercise. From San Francisco to the Islands would take over thirteen hours. No pilot had spent so much time in the air and none had flown two thousand miles over the sea. On September 19th, the first fourteen B-24s left San Francisco's Hamilton Field at dawn. Arthur Rogers flew in the lead plane. During the long flight he made several entries in his diary:

> *Our plan was to take off at dawn and circle the airdrome until all of the young pilots were in sight of us, and then strike out for the long distant land twenty-four hundred miles away. All of the ships were stocked with ninety days operations. We also had as much gasoline as we could carry. Our planes were exceedingly heavy for our take-off. I had never seen such a larger or crueler ocean than I saw at that time. After thirteen hours of flying and checking navigation we saw the large mountains of Hawaii. We were all relieved. Successful landing were made by all pilots. A tired but happy crowd was ready for bed after putting the planes away and taking their small belongings with them.*

Rogers counted all but one aircraft take off. He immediately assumed that one had had mechanical problems and had been towed off the runway. The reality was different. Lieutenant John Davis made a fuel-transfer error and his aircraft plunged into San Francisco Bay. All of the crew, except 2nd Lieutenant William Gunther, were rescued.

After nine days of guard duty, drills, cards, reading and tedium, the *Republic* sailed past Diamond Head into Honolulu Harbor before docking at Aloha Tower. The group's aircraft arrived in September and the squadrons began to reform. Members of the 321st were billeted at Wheeler Field, the 400th at Hickam Field and the 319th at

Kahuka. The men of the 320th never knew what they had done to deserve being stationed in a sugarcane field near Kipapa.

In his diary Walter Higgins summed up the group's activities during the next few weeks as 'training and more training'. He added, 'Flew some submarine patrols — sometimes 850 miles out — boring'.

On 21 September 1942, Arthur 'Tony' Speltz wrote a short letter home to his brother:

> *We had a nice trip over and the calm Pacific was beautiful all the way. Hawaii is a real paradise with swimming pools, golf course, tennis courts etc. Swam at Waikiki beach and ate at the Royal Hawaiian Hotel. Honolulu is a nice large city with streetcars, buses, Coca Cola and even hula girls. I have flown over the Islands several times, great from the air.*
> *Well must write Betty and Etta now so will close*
> *Your get-around brother*
> *Tony.*
> *P.S. In case you forgot my birthday is September 26 (just a hint).*

Speltz's family had not wanted him to enlist. His mother wanted him to stay with the family business, the one his dad had started in 1901. It was called the Speltz Grain and Coal Company and it was the biggest thing in the small town of Albert Lea, Minnesota. He listened when his brother, Stanley, told him not to get mixed up in the war: *It's the European thing all over again. America wants no part of it. Even Roosevelt is saying as much.* His sisters told him that he was needed in the company, but what did they know? He was the one who was expected to take over the business. His dad had been called Arthur too.

For the first time in his life Arthur Jnr had done something for himself. The family company — and their money — hadn't helped him one bit when he did his basic training at Bakersfield, or when he received his commission at Victorville. He was no longer Arthur

Speltz, clerk at Speltz Grain and Coal anymore; he was 2nd Lieutenant Arthur N. Speltz, United States Army Air Corps. It felt good.
He nearly burst with pride when he got his wings. 'It's a poor man
who doesn't look good in a uniform,' his mother had told him. The
Corps provided two uniforms — the guys called them pinks and
greens — but there was no need for the winter one in Hawaii. Everything fits him perfectly, except the flying boots; they're a little tight
and will have to be changed, but there doesn't seem to be any time —
anyway, the boots are made for flying, not walking.

He wished that his dad had been there to see him get his wings. It
had been ten years since he died. Now, Arthur had a new company —
Uncle Sam. He was co-pilot of a B-24 *Little Eva*. It was a good crew.
The skipper, Norm Crosson, was from Cincinnati and there was John
Dyer and Dale Grimes from Boston. The rest of the crew were okay,
mostly kids — Ed McKeon from New York, John Geydos from Ohio
and a goofy hillbilly called Gaston from somewhere in Alabama.

Arthur Speltz hung out with the other officers in the squadron and
was well liked. The guys called him Arthur, or Art. He didn't want
anybody in the Army to call him Tony — his family called him that.

The 321st was stationed at Wheeler Field, Oahu, next to Schofield
Barracks. Nobody could complain about the accommodation.
Arthur shared a residential billet with four other lieutenants. It had
four bedrooms, three bathrooms, and a fireplace. Shoot, it even had a
Frigidare. Nobody said that you had to do it hard, not like those poor
guys at Midway or New Guinea. Hawaii, what a posting. Compared
to his hometown of Albert Lea, it was paradise — beaches, swimming
pools, golf courses. It didn't worry him that he had no regular girl-
friend back in Albert Lea — there'd be plenty of time for that. He
didn't want any complications. He was too busy having a good time.
Some of the guys in the group were already married. Walt Higgins
got married the day he got his wings, sending his pay home every
week — nuts to that.

Arthur and his buddies went to Honolulu a couple of times. They played tennis and a little golf, but the big deal was Waikiki Beach. He wasn't much for the water, but Dale, he was one hell of a swimmer, a regular Johnny Weissmuller.

Norm Crosson's aircraft had been in the first wave when the group flew to Hawaii from San Francisco. Twenty-five hundred miles in one flight, under clear skies and over nothing but ocean. It had never been done before. There were six B-24s in the group, but Crosson's crew could have done it solo — John Dyer was the best navigator in the squadron.

Arthur had celebrated his birthday on September 26: twenty-six years old! The guys kidded him about that. Twenty-six was an old man in this war. A bunch of the guys took him on the town — what a night — starting at the Hawaiian and ending up at the Black Cat. You wouldn't know Hawaii was still under martial law. Everybody was having a ball. The pay was even better now Arthur was overseas. He was making nearly two hundred dollars a month; back at Albert Lea the job at Speltz Grain paid only fifteen hundred a year.

Most of the mail was from the family — birthday greetings and things. John Dyer got some records from the USO the other day. They were the new V Discs — Bing Crosby, Judy Garland and some swinging things by Tommy Dorsey and Cab Calloway. But the favourite disc was Artie Shaw's *Stardust* — it reminded everybody of home. Shaw was in the navy now and somebody said that Glenn Miller had joined the army. Everybody seemed to be doing their bit.

It had been nearly a year since the war started and nobody in the group had seen any action. They were a little green, but nobody doubted that, when the time came, they could dish it out. There had been something going on in the last couple of days, a couple of guys from the 320th had heard somewhere that the 90th was going to ship out again. Scuttlebutt was that it was either the Solomons or Australia.

The money was on Australia. Arthur didn't know much about the place, except that they were on our side and spoke English.

The paradise that was Hawaii was not to last. Between October 19th and November 1st, the Liberators and aircrews were on the move once again. This time the destination was Australia, 5000 miles away. The four squadrons were to fly via Christmas Island and Canton Island to the mysterious land down under. The ground echelon were to once again take an ocean voyage. The 90th Bomb Group also had a new leader. Colonel Arthur 'Art' Meehan took command on October 20th.

The reasons for the appointment of Meehan concern an issue that was deemed important enough to reach the attention of General Arnold in Washington. In a letter dated 8 October 1942, Arnold wrote to Major General Willis Hale in Hawaii:

We find ourselves faced with what may be a real and acute problem to psychology and in leadership in effecting a smooth and easy transition from the B-17 to the B-24. The net result is a false public impression that the B17 is a fighting aeroplane far superior to any other heavy bomber in the world, the B24 included, because of lack of briefness of combat experiences and publicity for its success in battle.

In the two-page letter, Arnold listed a number of features unique to the new Liberators. He concluded:

Your quick and careful attention must be given to the requirement that this popular notion of the inferiority of the B-24 shall not be reflected in the personnel of the 90th Bomb Group. It must be perfectly evident to you that the result might approach disaster if the 90th moves to Australia, replacing the splendid, but war-weary 19th, with the general belief that their airplane is an inferior weapon. I shall expect positive action on your part in this matter and will appreciate a letter from you stating the action taken and the results you will have attained.

On October 27th, Hale replied. His letter included a list of perceived shortcomings relevant to the B-24Ds. They included the forward gun installation, congestion in the nose, and no belly turrets. Hale suggested that the navigator be moved to a new position behind the pilot and that the forward guns installation be changed to allow much more field of fire. The belly turret would have to wait for a later model. Hale concluded:

The bulk of the personnel in the 90th Bomb Group, which are about to enter a war zone, are enthusiastic about entering the fight and have no feelings that the B-24 will not be satisfactory. The Group Commander and one Squadron Commander have been relieved.

The problems of acceptance for the B-24 had as much to do with aesthetics as mechanics.

American propaganda had elevated the B-17 Flying Fortress into an exalted warbird, indestructible and incomparable. Had they not flown MacArthur from the Philippines to Australia? Wasn't Charles Drake flying one in *Air Force*, a Warner Brothers film playing to capacity crowds in American theatres? It was sleek, powerful and all American. The B-24s were 'ugly sons of bitches'. For the young pilots it was like taking plain Jane to the prom. However, time would remove any doubts — the B-24s were more versatile, more resilient, could lift more and had a greater range. Before the end of the war more than one 90th aviator would owe his life to the squat-nosed buzzard from Consolidated.

From late October until early November the four squadrons of the 90th Bomb Group flew the vast distance of the South West

Pacific to Australia. The diary of Walter Higgins describes the odyssey:

October 26: *departed Wheeler Field to Christmas Island. Arrived same day. A plain atoll with some coconut trees and a few American troops.*
October 27: *Departed Christmas Island for Pago Pago. Met a bunch of marines and caught up with the war stories from Guadalcanal. It wasn't pretty, but we were winning. The marines were doing okay with the local babes. We are enthralled. The local beauties walk around bare-chested.*
October 28: *Pago Pago to Fiji. Saw some natives. The men have bushy heads and wear lap-laps.*
October 29: *Fiji to New Caledonia. Surprised to see the natives speaking French. One of my crew from Louisiana spoke fluent French. That seemed to send them into orbit.*
October 30: *New Caledonia to Amberley Field, near Brisbane, Australia.*

Australia was a mysterious land that few Americans knew about. The country had been at war since September of 1939. For the second time in a generation, Australia had leapt to the aid of Mother England in a European war and for the second time most of the best divisions were overseas fighting a foe that posed no direct threat. The Japanese menace in the Pacific was a different matter. In the early days of the Pacific War the Australians had suffered grievous losses. The fall of Singapore had led 18 000 men of the 8th Division into Japanese captivity. There was also a series of disastrous naval actions. On 19 February 1942, the same Japanese carrier task force that attacked Pearl Harbor bombed Darwin. It was the darkest hour — Australia had become the orphan of the South Pacific. Prime Minister John Curtin immediately ordered the 7th and 9th Divisions home from the Middle East. Churchill objected strongly but Curtin was adamant. The men were needed for home defence against the Japanese hordes. The only hordes that would invade the Australian homeland during the war were the American servicemen. They had been there almost since the beginning. A convoy of American ships that had been en route to the Philippines was directed to the Port of Brisbane after the Pearl Harbor raid. On 22 December 1941, the first Americans jumped ashore; hundreds of thousands more would follow.

In March 1942, General Douglas MacArthur arrived in Australia to take command of all Allied Forces in the South West Pacific area. Despite a botched defence of the Philippines, the flamboyant MacArthur was already a legend. A highly publicised escape by motor torpedo boats through Japanese lines only added to his heroic aura. MacArthur found the Australian people more than receptive to help from Uncle Sam. As early as December 1941, Curtin had told the *Herald* newspaper:

> *Without any inhibition of any kind, I make it quite clear that Australia looks to America, free of any pangs as to our traditional links of kinship with the United Kingdom.*

The Americans arrived in a vulnerable country that was in a perilous position; they were motivated not by Australia's needs but their own. The country offered the logistical and geographical advantages that would allow the United States to conduct the offensive against Japan. When MacArthur arrived in March, the number of US servicemen in the country totalled around 30 000. By the time the men of the 90th Bomb Group arrived in October, there were 120 000 Yanks posted down under.

The Americans had a difficult time coming to terms with the enigmatic Aussies. The country was the size of the United States, but the population was less than in New York. It was an isolated continent with an insulated culture. For the typical Australian the window to the outside world was the cinema, or 'the pictures'. The average Australian went to the pictures twice a week. The last film that Arthur Speltz saw before he left the States was *Western Union*. The first film he saw in Australia was *Western Union*. He wrote a letter home on November 3rd:

> *People are very nice here, but very odd. They talk funny and their English-type money is hard to get used to, using pound notes, shillings, pence etc. Cars are driven on the wrong side of the road and the steering wheels are on the right-hand side. The cars are all old 1921–1932. Myself and four other Lieutenants are looking at an old 1924 Dodge to buy but they want 60 pounds for it, which is about $235. It's too high. Women still wear longer dresses and have old-style hats. The Aussie soldiers wear shorts. There are cable cars in the middle of the road. Had a good time at a dance on Saturday night. Getting plenty of sleep. There are always plenty of mosquitoes cruising around.*
>
> *Plenty of cinemas here —* Babes on Broadway *is coming soon.*

Walter Higgins was also a curious observer of Australian culture:

> *… found the local people to be very hospitable. Their use of the English language was very interesting to a Texas lad. I went to a dance and the Aussie girls stayed on one side of the room and the boys on the other. In Brisbane, I went to get some money changed and saw an American girl. I could tell by her talk. She was a nice little thing and had a young boy with her. I was told that she was Jean MacArthur, wife of the General. His headquarters were now in Brisbane. We used to say that MacArthur was directing the war from his jungle headquarters in the bamboo room of the Brisbane Hotel.*

Grady Gaston was a young 22-year-old from Frisco City, Alabama. Like thousands of others, he had been drafted in 1941. A farm boy, he had never left home until the war. Soon after arriving in Australia, he wrote to his mother, Wattie.

This is a very big place with a lot of farms. Plenty of open spaces. All the folks are fine. I'm having trouble with the money. Pounds and pence. We don't know too much about the value. We usually just put some in our hand and tell the storekeepers to take what they want.

The posting of the 90th Bomb Group to Australia was ostensibly to relieve the 19th Bomb Group that was returning to the United States for regrouping. The 43rd Bomb Group, which had been in Australia since March, and now the 90th were the only heavy bomb groups available to engage the victorious Japanese. On paper the 90th looked a formidable force, but the reality was somewhat different. General Kenny, the commander of the 5th Air Force, was concerned enough to write to General Arnold:

Another disturbing element is the state of training of the B-24s coming from Hawaii. From the somewhat meager information I have to date I find that their night flying is not up to scratch. The job here calls for night take-offs with maximum loads and often with cross-winds climbing through overcast to fifteen to twenty thousand feet in order to navigate. I believe that considerably more night work is needed. I'm trusting that the tactical situation, the weather and other factors give me a chance to nurse them along for a while before I have to push them too hard, because they are not ready to start pitching the day they arrive in Australia by a long way.

The 90th did not stay long in Brisbane. The aircrews flew their aircraft to Townsville and then to a small rural community called Mareeba. The 'ground pounders' were still on the water coming from Hawaii and were not due to arrive in Townsville until November 24th. The squadrons regrouped in Mareeba and awaited orders. With crews assigned, the pilots began to give names to their ships — a popular tradition in all branches of the AAF.

Some of the names were inspired by popular songs: *Nobody's Baby, I'll Be Around* and *Pistol Packin' Mama.* Some were inspired by popular films: *The Powers Girl, Buck Benny Rides Again* and *Gone with the Wind*. Many were inspired by pretty girls: *Miss Ohio, Naughty Blue Eyes* and *Windy City Kitty*. James McMurria called his ship *Maid in the USA*. Walter Higgins named his B-24 *Cow Town's Revenge*.

The pilots were also allocated the crews that they would soon take into action. Norman Crosson's co-pilot was 2nd Lieutenant Arthur Speltz from Minnesota. The remainder of the crew comprised 2nd Lieutenants Dale Grimes and John Dyer from Boston, Staff Sergeants Loy Wilson, Charles Workman Jr and Corporal John Geydos Jr from Ohio, Staff Sergeant James Hilton from Texas, Edward McKeon from New York and Staff Sergeant Grady Gaston from Alabama.

The nose art on the 90th's ships was a serious business. Edward Jakowski was a 'ground pounder' of Polish origin, who was acknowledged as being the best artist in the group. Norm Crosson told him about a caricature he wanted painted on the nose of his B-24; it was to be of a very large woman riding a small motorcycle and had to reflect both mirth and menace. Crosson told Jakowski to caption the figure *Little Eva*.

CHAPTER TWO

'This place is the pits'

IRON RANGE is situated on a narrow finger of land at the north-east extremity of Cape York Peninsula. The area receives breezes from the Gulf of Carpentaria and the Torres Strait. There is no prolonged dry season. During the wet season the land has been known to receive 200 inches of rain in sixty days. It is remote and desolate and when overcast it is dark and forbidding. The site had been of interest to the military since the early days of the war. The RAAF believed that an all-weather airfield in the area could be useful.

Plans were drawn up for the project, with an estimated cost of £1500. No progress was made until April 1942 when an American aerial reconnaissance flown by Walter Maiersperger reported:

I had been ordered to make a survey of the coastal airfields of Queensland. On this trip I landed with the B-26 at Moresby, Horn Island and Coen and surveyed the area at Iron Range from the air only, as no construction had yet started there. All I saw from the air was the rainforest and the river winding down to the coast. It looked to be a promising site, but there may be logistical problems.

A few weeks later the American 46 Engineer Regiment began working on constructing two 7000 feet sealed runways and thirteen miles of sealed taxiways. The Americans called these two strips Gordon and Claudie. Heavy equipment, personnel and resources necessary for the project were dispatched to Portland Roads, a single jetty facility on the coast. Once unloaded, Caterpillar D8 bulldozers and D12 road graders cleared and widened the twelve miles of bush road to Iron Range. The American 46 Engineers and other ground echelon units did not easily forget the construction of the airfield in the Australian bush. Three camp sites each with 400 men laboured under arduous and primitive conditions to complete the project. As well as being demanding, the work was also dangerous. Work-related accidents were common. In September 1942, fourteen members of the 46 Engineers were stricken with ptomaine poisoning, better known as botulism. Six men from Company B and one from Company C subsequently died.

A report from the regiment to Base Section Three headquarters in Brisbane reflects the logistical and scheduling challenges confronting the engineers:

Iron Range progress report: Building mess hall operations — five room latrine — 12 capacity shower and wash all completed — water installations made. Field baker service available — butcher personnel present, herd en route. Strip 6800' complete and ready for landing although final surfacings not finished. Gasoline in drums available. Road 2 tracks graded from Portland Roads not complete but readily passable.

By November 1942, the 160-degree strip (Claudie) and a 120-degree strip (Gordon) were almost complete. Taxiways and bays were to be completed by December, weather permitting.

American aircraft began arriving at Iron Range before the dromes were even completed. The Gordon strip was still gravel when B–26 Marauders from the 19th Squadron of the 22nd Bomb Group landed on September 9th. Two weeks later the 33rd Squadron arrived. The 22nd Bomb Group were conducting operations — and suffering casualties — from Iron Range as early as September 13th. Only a week after Iron Range began operations, *Kansas Comet*, a B-26, under the command of Lieutenant Walt Krell, hit a termite mound, shearing off the right landing-gear strut. The aircraft lost control and crashed into a compressor truck parked on the western side of the strip. At this stage of the war several RAAF pilots were serving with the American squadrons. In addition to being an example of United States and Australian cooperation it also allowed many American co-pilots to leave their squadrons and train the ever-increasing number of new crews constantly arriving. Krell's co-pilot on this mission was Pilot Officer G. Robertson. After the collision with the truck, *Kansas Comet* lived up to its name and caught fire. Walt Krell suffered serious burns as he made a desperate effort to rescue Robertson, who died in the fire. A private from the 46th Engineers, R. G. Rodrigues, also died. It was a tragic accident, but it was only the beginning.

The dense jungle area of the base was useful for meeting camouflage needs, but it would also reveal major problems with large aircraft. The original strips had been designed for the B-26 Marauder, which had a wingspan of 65 feet. The clearing was 250 feet, a prudent distance for this type of aircraft. When the larger and heavier B-24 Liberators arrived, with a wingspan of 110 feet, no alteration was made. Aircraft manoeuvres at Iron Range would have challenged the most experienced pilots, a quality not yet attained by the crews of the 90th Bomb Group.

Some of the 90th Bomb Group's ground echelon had arrived in early November to prepare for the group's aircraft. The 319th, 320th and 400th squadrons arrived on November 13th. The forty-eight B-24 Liberators had been delayed in Mareeba due to faulty undercarriage nose wheels. It was no small task just to find Iron Range, which was virtually invisible from the air until you were over it. The 90th's pilots were already feeling trepidation about night operations. Crew members gazed out of the portals and could see the finished but still unsealed Gordon and Claudie strips. There were some clearings in the bush and what appeared to be tin sheds. Potential accommodation was obvious even from the air; pitched tents were strung between the trees. Many of the aircrews had heard scuttlebutt about the primitive latrines and mess areas. For the 289 officers and 1407 enlisted men of the 90th Bomb Group, Iron Range would be, by far, the worst posting of the war.

'Iron Range was the pits,' wrote Ernest Rhodes from the 319th. '… Right in the middle of the jungle. We lived in six-man pyramidal tents and had one large tent for a mess hall. It was hot and the weather for flying to Jap targets in New Guinea and New Britain was horrible.'

Only hours after their arrival at Iron Range, two aircraft from the 319th took off for a reconnaissance mission to Wewak, Madang, Finschhafen, Lae and Buna. It was an uneventful mission. Two days later, aircraft from the 319th and 400th staged the group's first bombing mission. The targets were Japanese ships in the Buin-Faisi anchorage of Bougainville Island. It was a daylight mission and the group was harassed by heavy anti-aircraft fire and Japanese fighters. Sergeant Clifford F. McCarthy, the tail gunner in Lieutenant Eckert's *8 Ball*, is credited with being the first member of the 90th to shoot down a Japanese aircraft in the war.

It was a disappointing mission, with negligible damage inflicted on Japanese shipping. The group suffered its first operational loss when Hank Werner's *Lady Beverly* ditched near the Island of Bia Bara. Only two of the crew, Lieutenant Walter C. Seidel and Sergeant Albert L. Butterfield, survived. Another Liberator, Dale J. Thornhill's *The Condor*, had damaged a wingtip while taxiing at Iron Range. After hasty repairs at Port Moresby the ship continued the mission, but because of the damage the crew were unable to conserve fuel. *The Condor* crash-landed on a beach near Iron Range; there were no serious causalities, only wounded pride. Three days later, the three squadrons were ordered to embark on a mission to bomb the large Japanese naval base in Rabaul, which had been captured by the Japanese in January 1942. It contained two excellent harbours, Blanche Bay and Simpson Harbour. There were also four airfields in or around the area. Defensive measures were formidable. A large Japanese fleet was in harbour and an army garrison of nearly 100 000 men; 367 anti-aircraft guns were operated by navy and army units.

The sortie to Rabaul was the first major test for the group. Fourteen aircraft were to depart from Iron Range beginning at 2300 hours. Rabaul was a distant 850 miles to the north-east. It was a long haul to a hot target. The aircraft were to set a north-easterly course across New Guinea and the Solomon Sea with the airspeed adjusted for an arrival over the target between 0400 and 0600 hours. It was all to be done at night. Most of the crews had yet to become familiar with Iron Range and no one had taken off in the dark.

The Liberators lumbered into position one hour before midnight. The noise was immense. Each ship was loaded with 2300 gallons of fuel and six 500-pound bombs. Squadron Commander Major Raymond S. Morse in *Punjab* took the lead position. Morse had only joined the squadron in Hawaii and barely knew the men under his command. His co-pilot for the mission was the group commander, Colonel Arthur W. Meehan, who had flown on the group's two previous missions. Meehan was a 38-year-old ex-West Point career officer who was in command of the 72nd Bomb Squadron the day the Japanese attacked Pearl Harbor. He had also been Assistant Chief of Staff for 7th Air Force operations before taking command of the 90th. Both Morse and Meehan were determined to lead from the front and it was from this position that *Punjab* took off from Gordon at 2300. As lead aircraft they took off with their landing lights on to aid the following aircraft. Morse climbed into the dark sky without incident, both he and Meehan were concerned as they circled the base. It was 2315 and the second aircraft had yet to depart. They could only assume that there must be problems below on the airstrip.

Leroy Iverson in *Big Emma* was to follow Morse, but he could not transfer fuel from his bomb bay tank. Cursing his predicament, Iverson was forced to abort the mission and leave the line. On board was another guest — Captain Robert S. Holt, the 320th's Intelligence Officer — and he was determined to partake in the mission. Leaving Iverson's ship, Holt ran towards Paul Larsen in *Bombs to Nippon* and motioned to him to open the hatch. Larsen would have none of it. He had enough to contend with. There was no time and there was no room. Larsen left Holt standing on the runway waving his arms. The incident was unfortunate and untimely, but it was a portent of what was to follow.

At 2310, there was considerable confusion. There was no means of communication with the crews. Some aircraft were not ready for take-off as scheduled. Others were reluctant to taxi out of sequence. There was only a limited amount of ground echelon and only a few wingmen. The runway lights were too far apart, and it was as black as a coal-mine.

Charles Andrews in *Change O' Luck* finally became airborne at 2314, the dust from his ship making vision even more difficult for Robert McWilliams in *Patches*. Slowly but unsurely others followed: Leo Campbell in *50 Cal Gal*, Charles Jones in *Dirty Gertie,* and Lieutenant John Wilson in *Tear-Ass,* a ship from the 320th and the ninth to leave the Gordon strip. Like Iverson, Wilson had another senior officer on board — Major Harry Bullis, Commanding Officer of the 400th Squadron.

Larsen in *Bombs to Nippon* throttled back and motored down the strip. As the ship gained momentum, his wingtip clipped the aborted *Big Emma*, tearing off the pilot tube and astrodome. Larsen lost control and the ship crashed into another parked Liberator. The aircraft immediately caught fire, with gasoline and bombs creating a massive fireball. Onlookers and medics rushed to help, but the fire was too intense. Larsen and his crew died, as did a lineman who had been sitting on the wing of the parked aircraft. A shocked and singed Robert Holt emerged from the holocaust alive but yet to appreciate his good fortune. Eleven men died and four aircraft were destroyed. The four remaining aircraft in line did not partake in the mission. It was a decision that disappointed no one. The airborne Wilson in *Tear-Ass* was told by one of his gunners that there appeared to be trouble back at the Range — big trouble, judging by the large red glow coming from the direction of the base. Wilson could see that it was the result of a fire. Someone suggested that it could be an air attack, but Wilson and Bullis knew immediately that there had been a collision. The night was already a disaster and most of the group was still on the ground.

Four hours later the squadrons approached the target on schedule, but clouds covered the harbour, creating poor visibility. Searchlights pierced the darkness followed by the crack of anti-aircraft fire. The aircraft dropped flares, which briefly revealed some large ships in the harbour. Campbell in *50 Cal Gal* dropped his load at 0420. Whitlock in *Cow Town's Revenge* circled the harbour for forty-five tense minutes before the bombardier shouted 'Bombs Away'. Nothing happened. A cursing crew member told Whitlock that *Cow Town's* bays had jammed with the bombs still aboard. This was a problem with the B-24 that would plague the group during the early months of the war. Two weeks later it would be a decisive factor in the fate of Norman Crosson and the crew of *Little Eva*.

Andrews in *Change O' Luck* was frustrated by the clouds and McWilliams in *Patches* could not find the target. Wilson in *Tear-Ass*, prompted by Major Bullis, concluded that there was a chance to improve visibility by flying under the clouds. Flying inland to manoeuvre for a run on the shipping, Wilson throttled forward and raced across the harbour at a height of 3500 feet with an air speed of 200 miles per hour. The bombardier, Lieutenant Weinberg, quickly aligned his Norden bombsight with what he believed to be a large destroyer or light cruiser. The crew swore that they observed a hit — there was fire and smoke. There were also hits on *Tear-Ass,* and leaks in the hydraulics forced the ship to detour to Port Moresby for repairs.

The raid on Rabaul by aircraft of the 90th Bomb Group did little to aid the prosecution of the war. There was frustration and ignominy. Damage to the enemy was slight, if not non-existent. McWilliams in *Patches* could not even find the target.

It was 0900 on November 17th when the first aircraft returned to Iron Range. There was so much wreckage and debris that the crews believed that there had been an air raid. It was a sombre base, even more so when the count revealed that two more aircraft were missing. *Tear-Ass* was located at Port Moresby, but there was no trace of *Punjab* with Morse and Art Meehan. Milne Bay and Port Morseby had heard nothing from them. The *Punjab,* 41-11902, and its crew of ten were never heard from again.

When Norman Crosson and the rest of the 321st arrived two days later, the base was still despondent from the disaster. There was no enthusiastic welcome. Crosson asked why there seemed to be so few aircraft on the base. It was then that he and the 321st were told that *Punjab,* with Morse and Meehan, was missing and all available aircraft were out searching.

Norman Crosson was solemn as he gathered his crew together. 'It's been a bad week up here. Hank Werner's ship went down near Bougainville, only Al Butterfield and Walt Seidel survived. Two nights ago, Paul Larsen's ship ran into Leo Iverson's. Larsen, Herb Bassman, Dave Muething, Diotti and Picker — the whole crew died in the fire.'

To the men of the 321st it was obvious that they were now at the business end of the war. Forget boot camp back at Barksdale Field, training at Greenville, flying from San Francisco to Hawaii, the fun in

Brisbane and the frolics in Townsville — Iron Range was the worst place in the world and men were dying.

The day before the 321st arrived, Colonel Ralph E. Koon was appointed new commanding officer for the 90th. The slight and slender, polite and taciturn forty-year-old had been a classmate of the missing Meehan. Both had attended West Point, Class of '28. Koon's sympathetic manner and firm but fair methods were not only desirable but also practical, particularly in a place like Iron Range. The transition was complete when Lieutenant Colonel Arthur H. Rogers replaced Ray Morse. Like all of the 90th, both men had no combat experience, but they were experienced officers. Koon had served at Langley Field before the war and both men had flown B-17s.

Although depleted of personnel the group conducted missions to New Guinea. On November 22nd, aircraft of the 321st led a night raid on Japanese installations on and near the Lae airfield at the mouth of the Huon Gulf. The first two aircraft dropped flares to illuminate the target. The next night four aircraft of the 400th delivered an encore. Damage was thought to be considerable, mostly to the runway.

The squadrons had flown direct from Iron Range to the target. The route was over the Owen Stanley Range — the setting for a desperate struggle between Port Moresby-bound Japanese and Australian AIF and Militia. The Japanese had been stopped and the tide had turned in favour of the Allies. By the middle of November the Japanese had retreated to the Buna and Gona beachheads, where another fierce campaign was being fought. Joining the Australians were men of the United States 32nd and 41st National Guard Divisions, who had moved up from their Australian bases in Brisbane and Rockhampton.

On November 29th, six aircraft from the 319th, led by Major Kuhl in Elmo Patterson's *Chosef,* attempted to locate and attack a flotilla of four Japanese destroyers that had been sighted making a dash from

Rabaul to Lae. Nobody could find the Japanese ships, but Ed DeFrietas in *Double Trouble* had become detached from the formation. Before heading for home he decided to perform a solo act on Lae. This target was a popular secondary choice for aborted missions and orphaned aircraft. Shortly after *Double Trouble* touched down on Gordon airstrip, the ground personnel started to arrive in trucks. The men had left Townsville in the old vessel *Cleveland Abbe*. It was scenic route travelling north inside the Great Barrier Reef. The majesty of the area gave no hint of what lay ahead. Like others before them, the ground crews were stunned into silence by the isolation and squalor of Iron Range.

Everyone could think of better places to be as they celebrated Thanksgiving. There seemed to be little to be thankful for. The men were kept busy. The officers' mess, surely among the most primitive and spartan in the Pacific, was completed. The enlisted men's mess was even worse. It was little more than a tarpaulin which served as a roof and furniture made from planks and drums. It was tolerable in fine weather, but impossible when the rains came. The ground crews were required to possess the virtue of improvisation. Parts were scarce. The damaged aircraft of the November 16th disaster were stripped for anything worthwhile. A detachment from the US 28 Service Squadron even went to strip Dale Thornhill's *The Condor*, which was still sitting on a beach five miles from the Range. In thirty-six hours they removed the engines, instruments and fittings; only the carcass remained.

Between missions the men faced the formidable challenge of finding something to do. Lieutenant Walter Higgins, when not behind the controls of *Cow Town's Revenge*, summed up the plight of the American aviators in the bush:

MacArthur forbade any booze in a lot of areas. That was no problem for the Air Corps. We bought footlockers and filled them. The Aussies had quart size beer bottles, but we loaded them up. We didn't worry about the

General. He was too busy at the best hotel in Brisbane running the war. We had as much as possible without women. We drank, explored the jungle, sang ribald songs often about the ancestry of the General and the Japs and anyone else that came to mind. Damm the snakes! We walked through the bush drunk or sober. We cursed the bully beef and hardtack, tea and what-ever else the cook served. The food chain at Iron Range was very rusty. Then we would sing another chorus of Roll me over in the Clover and do it again. We learned to sing Waltzing Matilda. No one knew what a billabong or a swagman was. We read and discussed our work, thought about home and wished the mail service was better. We even tried to build furniture out of the local bamboo and ironwood, to no end. It always fell apart and we would start all over — anything to keep busy. Jesus it was a terrible place. No good to visit. Even worse to live there.

James A. McMurria, a 26-six-year old pilot in the 321st, took a long look at his new home and environment:

There was no town, no village, no farmers, or ranchers that I ever saw living around Iron Range. There were some crude docking facilities in its sheltered harbor a few miles from the airstrip, but I never saw anyone tending it. Occasionally an ancient Australian barge of some dreary type would pull in there and a handful of Aussies would appear from the jungle and swap yarns with the crew until it moved quietly on. In the low areas dividing the hills were black pools of stagnant water. Huge trees stood in the middle of these pools much like our cypress, but their roots or knees were sometimes five feet above the water and extended themselves 10 or 12 feet toward the drier floor of the forest. To all of us it seemed like a 'Lost World' — unchanged for centuries.

Organised entertainment at Iron Range became a welcome respite from the pressures of war and the solitude of the posting. Colonel Koon introduced one outdoor epic in a solemn manner:

When we pause this day to recall all the things that we've done, the places we've been, and the fellows we've worked with, we do so not without remembering some of our buddies who are no longer with us. The memory of these men will always be mingled with high esteem and respect for their courage. Should any of us some day be called to join them in the same sacrifice for our beloved nation, their example would cause us to do so bravely.

These words were the only moments of solemnity in an otherwise joyful occasion organised during the bleak period of late 1942. A softball game between the 320th and the 321st started the spectacular at 1.00 pm. There was a ping-pong tournament, a volleyball match, and a horseshoe-throwing tournament that was dominated by the Texans. A band, which turned out to be a trio led by Corporal 'Lefty' Fowler, provided musical relief with songs of love warbled by Corporal Kerry O'Brien. But the big attraction was the evening movie. It was a battered 16 mm print of *Western Union*, which was flown in from Brisbane. The gala ended with a community singalong. The Army Air Corps song was an obligatory choice: 'Off we go into the wild blue yonder. Climbing high into the sun' was sung in mellow unison by the men. The final two bars were always bellowed with defiant enthusiasm: 'Nothin' will stop the Army Air Corps!'

The most anticipated entertainment was a letter from the States. The more the men read about home, the more they missed it. A portable phonograph and a collection of records were priceless items. Low-fidelity crooning by the Andrews Sisters, Bing Crosby and the Ink Spots were familiar sounds during liberty hours. The most popular recording was Benny Goodman's 'Jersey Bounce'; the shellac was soon worn off the Columbia single. Lieutenant William Krunz from the 320th squadron suggested that 'Jersey Bounce' would make a good name for one of the ships. Krunz was typical of many of the 90th's members who were blessed with improvisational flair but not always in the interests of Uncle Sam. He was one of the most successful foragers for liquor in the group, and he could also find women. When the 320th was in Mareeba, Krunz found a female companion in the nearby town of Atherton. Stranded with no transportation and the squadron due to fly out, Krunz bought a horse for £1, rode it back to Mareeba and turned it loose.

Mareeba and Atherton were quaint country towns with few facilities and little social activity, but they were Utopia compared with Iron Range. Bill Moran, a photo interpreter attached to S-2 in the group, arrived in mid-November:

> *It always seemed to be raining … mildew seeped into everything. the food was bully beef in every which way to cook. The coffee (?) was something else and what dehydrated foods we had were impossible to eat. Not far from us, the Aussie outfits had erected a bakery, in which they made bread … but not for us … the aroma from the bakery was mouth-watering.*

There were other Australians that were keenly observed by the Americans — the local Aboriginal people, who were often seen in close proximity to the base. The Aboriginals were an enigma to the Americans. Always aloof, the indigenous Australians impressed the visitors with their self-reliance and control of the elements.

Kangaroos, emus, bats, colourful birds, possums and the like were a constant source of fascination for the Americans, but other species were less appreciated. Few Yanks saw the feared crocodile — an animal not unlike the alligator found in the glades back home — but there was plenty of other wildlife to be wary of.

Most Yanks would have preferred to contend with the Japanese than suffer a confrontation with what seemed to be an endless variety of snakes, spiders and lizards. Most of the 90th Bomb Group members wrapped up in 'mummy'-like coverings at bedtime. A visit in the night by a creeping, slithering visitor was the stuff of nightmares. The most feared predator was the *Varanidae* (aka goanna), a veteran of the stone age, an essentially placid creature but visually terrifying. James McMurria recalled a close encounter with one:

> *Once on a short trek into the jungle for relaxation I saw a living object slither from the mud around a pond and then into the water. Someone shot it with a hand gun and fished it out with a long bamboo pole. It was horrible looking fish like the one whose picture you see in the dictionary with an unpronounceable name, not quite evolved from its prehistoric state. No one dared to touch it.*

He also recalled other encounters:

> *The wallabies we shot had the saddest eyes of all lonesome creatures in this lonely place, except for the eyes of the combat crews of the 321st Squadron.*

Walter Higgins never forgot the profusion of bird life on display.

> *It was fantastic — thousands of green parrots, white cockatoos, jackass birds and whatever. There was also the ever present kukaburro [sic]. We used to hear them all the time. I never knew an American during the war that could spell their name correctly.*

The nearest beach was five miles from the Range. The American strategy for fishing was often basic — using an outrigger canoe and blasting the fish with hand grenades. Bill Moran remembers that 'The Aboriginals on the beach with their fires generally got to retrieve and eat most of the fish'.

By December 1942 the Allies were beginning to mount campaigns to gain the initiative in the south-east Pacific. In mid November the Allies had begun offensives on the Japanese beachheads in Buna and Gona, but they had been repulsed and suffered heavy casualties. American forces were also engaged in desperate land, sea and air actions on and near the island of Guadalcanal in the Solomons. General MacArthur had temporarily moved his headquarters from Brisbane to Port Moresby. He was determined to secure the beachheads. MacArthur replaced General Edwin F. Harding, the field commander of the American 32nd Division, with General Robert Eichelberger, who had been posted in Australia with the US 41st Division. 'Go out there, Bob, and take Buna or don't come back alive,' MacArthur was reported to have said.

Eichelberger and the others knew that the Japanese were capable of landing reinforcements during the night. The day Eichelberger flew to Dobodura to take charge of all United States troops in the Buna area, the 90th Bomb Group was placed on alert. Two days earlier Colonel Arthur H. Rogers had arrived at Iron Range to undertake his role as Deputy Group Commander and Group Operations Officer. The aircraft had barely touched down from its flight from Christmas Island when Rogers was informed of a sighting of four Japanese destroyers en route to eastern New Guinea from Rabaul. Rogers and Koon quickly made plans to launch an attack on the Japanese ships.

At 0800 on December 1st, Rogers called a briefing for the group's squadron leaders. The operations room was a tin shack. The flight designations were crudely written on a large blackboard in the rear of the room. The men of the 90th thought that it resembled a bookie operation: the track, the rider, the horse and the race were the crew, the plane, the target and the time. Written on the board were the aircraft and the formations. No one referred to the aircraft by their serial numbers; instead the pilot's name was scratched on the board next to the name of his craft. Like the form of horses, the physical condition of the aircraft was written on another board. The engineers had the responsibility of updating the information. Richardson, *Seafood Mama* — 'faulty hydraulics'; Smith, *Naughty Blue Eyes* —'Nose wheel broke of'. When Hav Smith saw what was written beside his plane's name, he strode towards the board, saying, 'God damn! Where did the slide rule department get an education?' and he changed the 'of' to 'off'. It was the last time anyone laughed that day.

'The Japs could be going to reinforce their positions,' said Rogers. 'We're going to stop them.'

All of the squadrons were to take part and twenty-four aircraft would be involved — six per squadron. The formation would be in a triangle of a five-plane 'V', with one plane to close the triangle. The course would take them over the Owen Stanley Mountains to the Bismarck Sea and they expected to encounter the Japs south of Gasmata. If they got into any trouble they had the option of returning through Port Moresby.

For the men of the 90th Bomb Group, the strips at Port Morseby became almost as familiar as Iron Range.

Walter Higgins recalled:

It was an important stop either going or returning from missions. We used to approach Port Moresby by circling over an old German hulk that had been on the reefs at Moresby since the first war. We then went to our landing strip. The 90th used the Ward strip. On occasion we would use the Jackson strip. The area was often hot with the Japs attacking the facilities.

In the tin shack at Iron Range the airmen conducted a 'time-tick': a routine of synchronising their watches to the official times. Crosson was keen to get under way.

After more specific briefings from intelligence, armament and weather officers, the men were given their individual assignments and then dispersed in order to brief their crews. This was to be one of the most ambitious missions undertaken since the group arrived in Australia. All of the squadrons were to take part. Few of the 90th Bomb Group's 1696 men at Iron Range were not involved in some capacity. Arthur Speltz found time to write a short letter to his mother and his sister Peggy:

I had a big Thanksgiving dinner — turkey, potatoes, carrots, pickles, fruit salad and ice cream. We invited the base priest for dinner but he was going turkey and alligator hunting. Bill and I went to Mass and Communion on Sunday. Not too much to do here but rest and sit in our club. We built a new club and got a radio. We can pick up Tokyo. They give us quite a program and to hear it you would think they were winning the war.

At 1200, Crosson, Speltz and the other crew members climbed into the Dodge truck to be ferried to the area where *Little Eva* awaited. Crew chiefs had already loaded the ordnance and gasoline. The two pilots, together with James Hilton and two crew chiefs, began a walk-around inspection of the aircraft. Crosson, always methodical, instructed Hilton to climb on the wings to check that the gas caps were secure. It was a Davis wing, an ideal heavy-duty structure. The fuel gauges were also checked. The visual inspection complete, the *Little Eva*'s men were told to board. The procedure was to enter through the bomb bay, which was no easy task with a full kit. As well as a parachute, most wore a steel-reinforced vest as protection against flak splinters and a bulky flight suit to protect against the zero temperatures at high altitude. All carried a steel helmet and an oxygen mask that was never comfortable: 'It felt like a clammy hand clutching the lower part of your face,' said one airman.

Crosson and Speltz strapped themselves into the pilots seats — dual controls side by side — flanked by instrument and windscreen panels, compass and control wheel housings. Seated behind the pilots, opposite the emergency escape hatch, sat the radio operator, Staff Sergeant Grady Gaston. Lieutenant John Dyer, the navigator, was positioned in front of the pilots, segregated in his swivel seat by the forward mainframe bulkhead. The astrodome, mounted in the top section, provided a full 380 degrees observation. Forward of Dyer was the domain of Dale Grimes, the ship's bombardier. Flight Engineer Hilton's station was behind the fuselage mainframe bulkhead. He was in charge of all things mechanical. In the advent of him becoming indisposed,

McKeon, the assistant engineer, would fill his role. McKeon also manned one of the manually operated .50 inch waist guns. This station was situated in the middle of the ship, beyond a catwalk through the bomb bay leading to the after fuselage — a robust section of the aircraft containing an aluminum alloy structure with five main bulkheads. Assistant radio operator Loy Wilson manned the other waist weapon. Charles Workman operated the two-gun dorsal turret. John Geydos manned the .50 calibre twin gun in the 'blister'-shaped, electronically operated tail turret; known throughout the force as 'Tail End Charlie', this was a lonely, dangerous station.

The operation started at 1330. The 319th Squadron was the first into the air. Colonel Rogers and Major Phillip Kuhl, who were flying with Lieutenant John R. Arant in *Pretty Baby*, left the runway first. The Liberators of Lieutenants Robertson, Rice, Jones, Weber and Currie soon followed the Group Commander. Major Harry J. Bullis followed with six ships from the 400th Squadron. Crosson began checking his flight controls until he was satisfied they worked freely. His crew checked the bomb load, radio, navigational instruments. All was well. Crosson and Speltz opened the cowell flaps and set the throttle at a third. He set the mixture controls to full rich. With the gasoline pump on, the starter was energised and, when it reached sufficient power, the pilots started the engines. Number three engine was first — it contained the hydraulic source. Number one, number two and number four engines roared to life in sequence. The crews enjoyed the sound of the Pratt & Whitney R-1830–43's twelve hundred horsepower; they were exhaust-driven, supercharged and reliable. Most pilots believed them to be superior to the B-17's Wright engines. With the engines in harmony, Crosson signalled the crew chiefs to remove the front and rear wheel chocks and pressed the throttle forward. *Little Eva* began moving towards the take-off position.

Crosson ordered the bomb bay doors closed, trailed the engine flaps and adjusted the hydraulically operated Fowler wing–flaps to ten degrees. He ran the engines up one more time and checked his magnetos. The r.p.m. was good. Crosson and Speltz watched as the 321st began to move in formation. Major Cecil L. Faulkner was in the lead, followed by the aircraft of Lieutenants James J. Crawford, Walter E. Higgins, James A. McMurria, George M. Rose and Crosson. The ships were moving thirty seconds apart, taxiing down the runway like 'a gaggle of geese going to a pond'.

When Rose started his take-off, Crosson focused his eyes on the tower to await the green light. 'Wait for it, wait for it' — 'Okay, it's us,' he said. With twenty-degree flaps and maximum mercury, Crosson released the brakes and *Little Eva* began its journey. Crosson eased back the pressure on the nose gear and watched his airspeed — 80, 90, 100, 110 mph. The revs were 2800. The ship raced along the rough Gordon tarmac. The engines roared, the aircraft shuddered, and there was a period of calm as Crosson throttled back and 60 000 pounds of aircraft became airborne. The men took a breath and braced themselves. No matter how many missions anyone flew, it was always a relief to get off the ground. At 400 feet Crosson reduced the power to 25 inches of mercury and the r.p.m. to 2550. At 600 feet the r.p.m. was 2350. The main wheels were retracted into the wells on the underside of the wings, the nose wheel backwards into the front fuselage. The wheels and flaps were taken up and the aircraft began to climb into formation. The crew could see the ships of the 400th and 319th up ahead. Those of the 320th were preparing to leave Iron Range. Geydos in the rear turret watched as the last two ships took off and the base, the area and then the continent disappeared over the horizon.

The group gathered in formation without incident. Crosson asked for a report from the crew on the intercom. All was well. Dyer checked his course settings and Grimes released the string triggers on the eight 500 lb bombs. It would take about four hours to reach the Gasmata area. The weather was overcast and cloudy. Ahead for the

twenty-four Liberators of the 90th Bomb Group was the deep purple
of the Coral Sea and then the grey-green mass of the Owen Stanley
Mountains. Beyond that lay danger and destiny.

CHAPTER THREE

'Where's Norm Crosson?'

SOMEONE once said that operational flying was 95 per cent boredom and 5 per cent terror. No one in the four squadrons flying to the target on that first day of December in 1942 would disagree. It was a long, tedious journey over the ranges of New Guinea. The crews knew little about the Owen Stanley Mountains and the fierce battles of attrition that had taken place there from July to October. Australian units had encountered and stalled a force of crack Japanese troops determined to capture Port Moresby. The smoke had cleared from the battle and the Japanese had retreated to bunker fortifications on the island's north-east coast.

From the air the Owen Stanleys looked ancient and sinister. The place to observe them was definitely from the air. No one wanted to think about coming down somewhere in the mountains. To most observers it was 'creepy and spooky'. On this December day, vast expanses of the mountains were obscured by intermittent cloud cover. The group's formation — the 319th leading, followed by the 400th, the 321st and the 320th — was predetermined, with the crews most familiar with the route leading the formation. The navigators of the 319th plotted the course for the others to follow.

Crosson was eager to give a good showing. It was the *Eva's* first

mission and this was the biggest group sortie thus far in the war. He
had an eager but inexperienced crew and this was the moment that
they had trained and prepared for. He had told them so during the
flight. The intercom buzzed with motivational fervour and a call to
duty. Crosson ran a tight ship, but he also knew the benefit of good
morale. The crew were allowed to smoke when the ship was flying at
less than 7000 feet, and they were allowed to chatter providing no one
took his eye off the ball. When Crosson learnt that Gaston had some
fresh fruit and Workman some candy, he permitted them, in turn, to
pass the snacks around the ship. It was no big deal, but it pleased the
crew.

Crosson gazed at Major Faulkner's ship in the front of the
squadron. *Eva* was to the left and Higgins in *Cow Town's Revenge* flew
on the right flank. McMurria, Rose and Crawford's ships were in the
middle. It was not just Crosson's crew that was about to be tested, but
also the whole squadron. Faulkner wanted the 321st to be the best
squadron in the group. It was 1800 hours and the weather near the
north-east coast of New Guinea was much clearer. Rogers, leading
the 319th, changed course to run down the slot in the Bismarck Sea
between New Britain and Finschhafen. He did not want to experience the ignominy of not finding the Japanese destroyers — always a
distinct possibility. At 1810 there was no more doubt: 'Ships bearing
south-east of Gasmata, about thirty miles … one, no three … wait,
there's more'. The bombardier in Chuck Jones's ship had seen them
first. Other eyes brought confirmation. They had found them.

The Japanese had entered World War II with a poor sense of operational logistics. The swift victories in the early months of the war had
created vast areas of conquest and equally distant garrisons. Supplying
stores and reinforcements to isolated areas was to become a problem
that would ultimately become a crisis. The Japanese merchant fleet,
whose task it was to ferry stores to and from the areas of occupation,
were gradually being decimated by a rejuvenated American

submarine service. The battle for Guadalcanal was the first campaign of the Pacific War to be decided by operational logistics. Despite having considerable forces deployed in the conflict, the Japanese were totally unable to land sufficient stores or reinforcements on the island.

The American airstrip on the island proved decisive, with the 'Cactus Air Force' taking full toll of surface shipping en route to supply the Japanese garrison. Japanese 'Marus' littered the seas and shores of Guadalcanal. By November, the Japanese were using destroyers loaded with stores to run the gauntlet at night, rolling steel drums from the decks to land on the beach with the tide. It was too little and too late.

The beachheads at Buna and Gona, where the Japanese were preparing to make a last stand, represented a similar situation to that confronting the strategists at Guadalcanal. On 17 November 1942 the Japanese successfully landed another 1000 men at Buna. By the end of the month the garrison totalled 8000. Regular supplies from Rabaul became a life or death matter for the Japanese. The destroyer convoy due to arrive in Buna on December 2nd would be a welcome boost to the fortunes of the garrison. It had departed Rabaul two days earlier and the journey had so far been uneventful, but at 1830 hours on December 1st, 200 miles south of Gasmata, vigilant lookouts on the destroyers sighted an American bomber formation to the north-east.

Rogers' plan was for each squadron to independently make two passes, which would effectively double their chances of hitting the small moving targets. The problems were apparent. It would take longer to complete the mission and would afford the Japanese time to further prepare and also increase the possibility of a confrontation with Japanese fighters.

The Mitsubishi *Zeke* was the most successful Japanese fighter aircraft of the war. In the early days of the Pacific conflict it reigned supreme, but by the end of 1942 the Americans were beginning to understand the strengths and weaknesses of the aircraft they referred to as the 'Zero'. The type that flew operations in the south-west Pacific theatre from late spring 1942 was the A6M3. Its 1130-horse-power engine provided speed and manoeuvrability at the expense of armoured protection. The 10 938 Zeros built during the war were armed with twin 7.7 mm machine guns, synchronised to fire through the airscrew, and 20 mm cannons mounted in the wings. They could fly in excess of 300 miles per hour at 20 000 feet. One feature that concerned the Americans was a climbing rate of 3000 feet a minute.

The men of the 319th Squadron were alarmed but not surprised to observe fifteen Zeros in the vicinity of the convoy. Like swarming bees they began racing in the direction of the Liberators. Rogers knew that the best way to do battle with Zeros was to maintain formation and use organised and concentrated firepower. He had six ships in his formation; the other squadrons were still a considerable distance to the rear — too far behind to have an impact in the early stages of the battle to come.

'Maintain "V" formation,' said Rogers. 'They'll attack from the front — they always do.'

Rogers was correct. The Japanese flew over and ahead of the squadron and turned to conduct a frontal attack on the American bombers. It was a typical 'string formation', one fighter at a time flying and firing at the B-24s in an attempt to break up the formation. Rogers' crew fired first with the two nose fifties. Soon the other ships opened up; waist and tail gunners fired at the Zeros as they over-flew the formation. Strict formation also helped with the accuracy of the gunners. The dorsal and rear gunners were restrained in their blisters, but the waist gunners had no such restraint. However, a level ship flying in formation enabled them to maintain steady and accurate fire. The frontal attacks at a combined closing speed of 500 miles per hour was a terrifying experience, particularly for the ship's bombardier, encased like a fish in a bowl and preoccupied with getting a fix on the target. It was no less terrifying for the Zero pilots when confronted with a concentrated wall of fifty-calibre amour-piercing rounds. One Zero was caught in a turn and hundreds of fifty-calibre rounds blasted into the unprotected belly tank. The Zero crashed into the sea in flames. When flying in formation, the credit for kills was always a contentious issue for crews. On this day it was Rogers' ship that claimed first blood.

The 319th maintained a steady formation and began the first bomb run at 15 000 feet. It was no easy task. The Zeros were still hovering and pestering the formation and the anti-aircraft fire from the destroyers was becoming more concentrated. The squadron's bombardiers kept cool heads and began to align their Nordens.

The development of the Norden Bombsight was begun in 1928 by inventor Carl Norden and engineer Theodore Barth. It was a radical new aiming device that was linked to the aircraft's autopilot. The bombardier entered data on air speed, wind and bomb trajectory, and, as the bombardier aligned the lens to the target, the Norden automatically released the bombs at the proper release point. It could 'drop a bomb into a pickle barrel from 25 000 feet', boasted the United States Air Corps. The stringent secrecy surrounding the device, and the regard for it, was not inspired by performance. At best, during clear weather, the Norden could direct one in five bombs within 1000 feet of the target.

The existence of the bombsight remained classified until 1947. The American military was paranoid about it falling into enemy hands. During the Doolittle raid on Tokyo in May 1942, the Americans removed the Nordens from the B-25 Mitchells and left them on the USS *Hornet*.

The value of the Norden against shipping in the Pacific theatre was suspect. Despite the crushing victory by the American navy over the Japanese in the battle of Midway, a squadron of B-17s from the island could not claim a single hit on the large Japanese fleet, in perfect weather conditions. Moreover, a confidential report submitted to the

American military revealed that only one in a hundred bombs dropped by high-altitude bombers on enemy shipping hit the target. One pilot from the 90th suggested that he would be happy to trade the Norden for an extra gallon of gas.

The first run on the destroyers achieved nothing, not even near misses. The second run was better; a hit was observed on the stern of one of the destroyers. Rogers noticed that the ships of Jones and Rice were in trouble. Smoke was pouring from their starboard engines. They would need to get the crippled ships back to Port Moresby at the double. Fortunately for the squadron, the Japanese Zeros had departed — doubtless short of fuel and ammunition. The 319th squadron claimed to have made five kills during the engagement, an ambitious and unlikely figure which was never confirmed.

No sooner had the squadron set course for Port Moresby than the remaining squadrons prepared to engage the enemy. It was easy to find the ships; not only had their position been given but the crews could see the ominous signs of anti-aircraft fire in the distance.

Light was fading as the 321st gathered to make a bomb run on the ships. McMurria led a three-ship formation with Higgins on the left and Crosson on the right. The anti-aircraft fire had eased, but it was still hot. It was possible that the Jap fighters would come back. Nobody wanted to hang around; everybody wanted to hit and run. Tom Doyle, the bombardier in McMurria's ship, shouted into the intercom, 'I think we've hit one — on the stern. I think she's slowing down.'

Crosson was next. This was it — the crew was at last in action. 'I'll hold her steady, Dale,' said Crosson. 'Make 'em count.'

Grimes lined up the Norden, slowly and surely. 'Wait, wait … hold it … wait … steady … bombs away.' There was a moment of silence and then Grimes was once again on the intercom: 'God damn it!'

'What's the matter?' shouted Crosson. 'Dale, what's the matter?'

'They've hung up,' said Grimes. 'The bombs have hung up. There's something wrong with the racks.'

'Jesus Christ! Try and fix it — we'll try one more run,' said Crosson, already thinking the worst — an ignominious mission failure.

It was no better the second time. *Eva* was forced to leave the formation. The aircraft of the 320th were forming in the rear to attack. Crosson pulled out of line. Grimes left his station and inspected the rack and made some adjustments. Minutes went by.

'It should be okay now, Lieutenant,' said Grimes.

'It's too late for the ships,' said Crosson. 'We've missed our chance.'

Crosson had two options. He could drop his ordnance into the sea and return to base with the squadron, or he could break formation and attack the secondary target, which was Lae, less than one hour's flying time away.

The Japanese had occupied Lae in March 1942. The Allies were surprised that the Japanese had not moved inland. Instead they formed a garrison which became a popular raiding target for RAAF and American aircraft. In the month of August alone, the Allies flew fifty-six sorties and dropped 150 000 pounds of bombs on Japanese installations.

'We're goin' to visit the Japs at Lae,' Crosson told his crew on the intercom. 'We'll drop our load and be back at the base with the others later tonight.'

Crosson could sense the crew's disdain through the intercom. He had no doubt that they would prefer to follow the squadron home. A one-ship raid on Lae was likely to be a waste of time and was definitely a considerable risk, particularly as the bombs might still be hung up.

Crosson was determined to proceed with his plan. He consulted with Faulkner and received permission to break formation. He told Dyer to plot a course and turned his ship to the south-west. Dyer acknowledged, but then informed the lieutenant that there appeared to be some storm activity on the horizon.

For the crew of *Little Eva* the flying adage of boredom versus terror was about to be reversed.

The closer that *Little Eva* got to Lae, the closer the storm enveloped them. It was still thirty minutes to target when Crosson decided to abort the mission. The sky was black, there were flashes of thunder and there was little doubt about the potential danger that lay ahead. Crosson told Grimes to drop the bombs into the sea. The crew grimaced — yet another failure and more ignominy.

Little Eva was above the Solomon Sea, alone and off-course. Ahead lay the Owen Stanley Range, but Dyer and Crosson could not see the mass. Dark clouds and the approaching night were obscuring the area. Crosson and Speltz would have to fly on instruments. Although instrument-flying was considered routine, few pilots had experience and the standards were variable. The strategy was simple: fly a couple of thousand feet above the highest mountain in your path and add a few more thousand to be sure. Forget 'flying by the seat of your pants'; it was a poor flight indicator, and the inner ears gave a false sense of balance. 'Always use the artificial horizon,' said the instructors. 'Needle and ball, airspeed and compass — it works.'

Timing was also important. The clouds were always a little lower in the morning, getting higher as the day progressed. Most aircraft flew the route from Port Moresby down to Hood Point and over the mountains. There were two good reasons — the mountains were not quite as high in this area and the base wanted constant weather updates in the area. But Crosson did not have the luxury of timing and the weather conditions were ominous. Soon fierce winds and heavy rain were hitting the ship.

Flying directly into a tropical storm was the stuff of nightmares. Winds could reach 200 miles per hour. Crosson and Speltz were flying to stay alive. The ship could fall apart at any moment — *Eva* rattled and shook. The other crew members became observers; some prayed; all were terrified. For nearly an hour *Eva* was like a metallic leaf in the fierce wind. Crosson attempted to fly around the storm and then to fly above it — 20 000 feet would do it — *Eva* could not climb that high. The crew members were impressed by the ability of Crosson and Speltz to fly the ship in such conditions. Gaston told McKeon that they might just make it after all.

'We're goin' to get outa' this,' he said. 'The skipper's getting on top of the storm. It's goin' to be all right.'

Suddenly, all hell broke loose. *Eva* flipped and plunged towards the earth. Those not restrained were thrown around the ship like pickles in a barrel. The aircraft was in a spin — a potential disaster for any pilot, and even more so in a tropical storm.

'Hold tight! Hold on to something. We're going down,' yelled Crosson.

The leaf was now like a top spinning towards oblivion. Speltz began to call out the altitude. 'Nineteen thousand … seventeen thousand … sixteen thousand … do something … fifteen thousand … fourteen thousand … do something. For God's sake, do something.'

As Speltz blessed himself, more than one man began to cry.

Crosson remembered an old procedure that he had learned in primary flying school. With enough altitude, it just might work. He had no choice; it was do or die. He cut the power to the engines and neutralised the controls. The stick went forward and Crosson kicked the rudder in the opposite direction. The ship shuddered even more than in the storm.

'Thirteen thousand … thirteen-five-hundred … What are you doing? You'll knock the damn wings off,' said a terrified Speltz.

Crosson knew that a stalling ship would shudder as it entered the stall. The ship should drop to the left due to the torque of the spinning props. As the nose dropped, Crosson kicked full right rudder and reapplied power. The crew could sense the stress on the wings, but they were the Davis type — the toughest in the world. Rivets popped and the fuselage shook, and moments became minutes. The crew were about to brace themselves for the inevitable when *Eva* began to resume level flight. It was a minor miracle and the only thing to go right for Crosson's crew since the mission began.

'Jesus Christ, we did it. You can't do that with a four-engine job,' said Speltz.

'Go tell that to the Consolidated Aircraft Company,' replied Crosson.

The spin was not the end of their troubles; it was just another episode in their ordeal. The weather was a little clearer over the Coral Sea, but not clear enough for celestial navigation, and the instruments had been rendered useless by the severity of the storm.

'John, have you got a fix on where we are?' asked Crosson. 'Can anybody see the light?'

Iron Range was tough enough to find during the day, but at night it was even worse, especially with the dust and the cloud cover. The field sent up a vertical searchlight that could be seen for miles; once crews located this, the landing lights would guide them in.

The radio operators on the B-24s sent routine communications to the base while on missions or on recon. Gaston's reports to the base were becoming desperate. He gave an estimated position provided by Dyer, but it did not inspire confidence. After a spin-out most navigators became confused and disoriented. One said that you couldn't find 'your ass with both hands'. The tower always knew the routes that missions flew; however, *Eva* was anywhere but on the official route.

'I think we've missed the base,' said Dyer. 'We should be on the east

The Dude and *Eager Beaver*, B–24D Liberators similar to *Little Eva*. Note the 90th Bomb Group skull and cross bomb insignia on the tail section of *Eager Beaver*.

The complex cockpit of a B–24D Liberator. Note the automobile style control columns.

A date with destiny — the Gasmata mission, 1 December 1942, photographed from the waist-gunner's hatch.

Arthur Speltz the aviator, and (above) in dress uniform.

The *Little Eva* wreck site. This is how Ian Hosie would have viewed the elusive crash site on the morning of December 16, 1942.

Sergeant 2nd Class Heinrich 'Harry' Nuss — officer in charge of the Burketown Police Station 1942.

Burketown, circa 1940. Ian Hosie of the Flying Doctors landed his Tiger Moth on the main street. The police station is the building in the centre foreground.

The wet season with storm clouds gathering. Photographed from the rear of the Burketown Police Station.

Wilson and Crosson recovering from their ordeal, Burketown, December 1942.

Bob Hagarty —
'as tough as nails'.

Hagarty on horseback on the trail, complete with his long-blade sheathed knife.

The Gregory Downs Police Station.

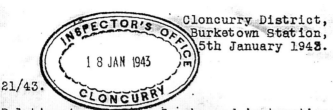

Cloncurry District,
Burketown Station,
5th January 1943.

INSPECTOR'S OFFICE
1 8 JAN 1943
CLONCURRY

21/43.

Relative to:- Plane Crash, and instructions given to
Constable Marsh, and interviews and information
obtained from Pilots Crossan and Hosie. Vide your
telegram on the 4/1/43.

18/1/43

Sir,
    I have to report that on the 4th Instant, I received
the following telegram from the Inspector of Police,
Cloncurry, in connection with the plane crash on
Moonlight Creek on or about 2am on the 3rd December 1942

        Sergeant Nuss,
        Burketown.

Furnish full report relating Plane crash giving your
instructions Const Marsh, interviews and information
obtained from Pilots Crossan; Hosie subsequent action
taken by you why search discontinued when Police
Party in locality plane.

        Galligan.

Senior Inspector Galligan was less than happy with the progress of the search for *Little Eva*.

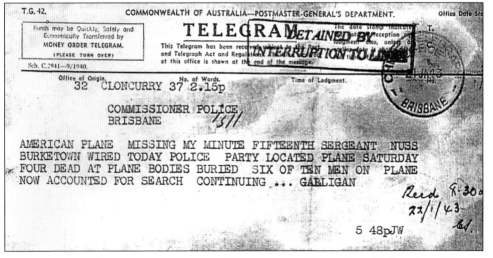

T.G. 42.   COMMONWEALTH OF AUSTRALIA—POSTMASTER-GENERAL'S DEPARTMENT.   Office Date Sta

Funds may be Quickly, Safely and
Economically Transferred by
MONEY ORDER TELEGRAM.
(PLEASE TURN OVER)
Sch. C.2941—9/1940.

TELEGRAM

This Telegram has been received subject to the Post
and Telegraph Act and Regulations.
at this office is shown at the end of the message.

DETAINED BY INTERRUPTION TO LINE

Office of Origin.   No. of Words.   Time of Lodgment.
    32 CLONCURRY 37 2.15p

COMMISSIONER POLICE,
BRISBANE

AMERICAN PLANE MISSING MY MINUTE FIFTEENTH SERGEANT NUSS
BURKETOWN WIRED TODAY POLICE PARTY LOCATED PLANE SATURDAY
FOUR DEAD AT PLANE BODIES BURIED SIX OF TEN MEN ON PLANE
NOW ACCOUNTED FOR SEARCH CONTINUING ... GALLIGAN

Recd 8.30
22/1/43

                                                        5 48pJW

The Queensland Police commissioner, C.J. Carroll, receives news that *Little Eva* has been located.

C.J. Carroll, Queensland
Police Commissioner.

Bob Hagarty's expert and detailed
drawing of the wreck site, which he
included with his comprehensive report.

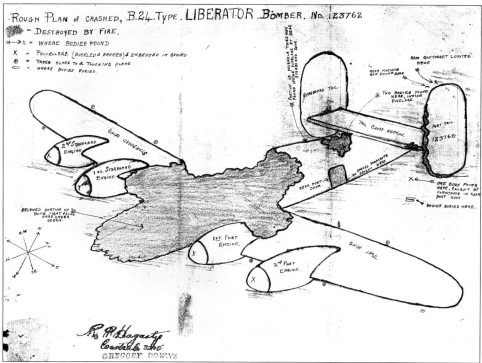

coast, heading south, maybe 100 miles from Cairns. Should we continue our present heading?'

Crosson throttled back to conserve fuel and he reduced altitude. Flares were dropped in the hope of identifying some distinctive topographical features, or perhaps of getting some response, but they revealed only darkness and desolation. Helpless at their stations, the crew were in a state of fear. When Crosson instructed Gaston to send a mayday, the fear became terror.

The storm that had tormented *Little Eva* had also spread to the Gulf country. Frank Walden at Escott Station watched the gathering of clouds become dark and threatening. Since early evening on the 1st it had rained. It was always the same at this time of the year. First it would sprinkle and then it would come down by the bucketful. It was the start of the 'wet'. Walden liked the sound of rain. After months of parching heat and dry fields, it was a welcome respite. Soon the gullies and creeks would overflow and the parched land would be enveloped in water. The station's business was cattle and the cattle had to have fresh feed. The 'wet' brought new challenges, but it was a more desirable protagonist than drought.

Escott Station was one of the oldest properties in the Burketown area. Legend has it that a man called Nat Buchanan walked the first cattle into the area in 1864. Four years later, the land was owned by the English, Scottish and Australian Pastoral Company. The name 'Escott' came from this commercial alliance. Gulf fever claimed the life of the manager of the station and the property was abandoned. In the last decade of the century, the property was sold to the Walden family.

The original homestead had been built on the 'Old Marless' station, which represented 90 per cent of the property. In 1934, the fifty-year-old homestead was destroyed by fire. The Walden family rebuilt at Escott and moved into their new home in 1942. The station covered a massive area, stretching from the Albert River to the

Northern Territory and up to the Gulf. It was estimated that the area was about 250 000 acres. It would take a week to ride from one boundary to another.

The Walden family listened to the war news through a short-wave radio. Although the reception was as bad as the news, it was the family's window to the outside world. The arrival of the Americans, at first seldom acknowledged, was a source of comfort to the people of the outback. The threat of invasion was still real for the people of the 'Top End'; any Japanese offensive would undoubtedly start there or on the North Queensland coast. The distant engine noises of American aircraft, mission-bound for New Guinea, or returning to their northern bases, were a comforting sound on a quiet night.

Frank was lying awake in the early hours of 2 December 1942 when he heard the engine sound of a heavy bomber, away in the distance but getting closer. There was something odd about the aircraft — not the sound but the direction it was coming from. It wasn't like the others he had heard. Frank lit a lantern and walked to the front verandah. Soon he was joined by his wife, Ellen.

'What is it, Frank?' she asked.

'I dunno. It's a plane, but I think that it's heading west. Maybe it's lost. It sounds like it's close and low … Sshh … Don't you hear it? It's coming from the east … listen.'

'I don't hear anything. Why would it be going west? It's probably just thunder.'

'No, it's a plane. I can tell.'

'It could also be a Jap plane,' said Ellen. 'Better put out the lantern.'

Frank looked in the direction of the sounds. He saw a quick flash — or was it a light, maybe a signal or a beacon? — but then he could see nothing. The sound grew distant. There was no doubt it was heading west, but why? There was nothing out there, nothing at all. The rain grew heavier and there was the odd flash of lightning. Frank put out the lantern and went back inside. It had been a long day. He fell asleep to the sound of rain falling on the tin roof.

Crosson knew that time was running out. The gauges told the story. There was no more than 100 gallons in each tank — enough for twenty minutes flying time. 'John, where are we? For God's sake, do you have any idea where we're going? Unless we bring her down soon, we'll have to jump.'

'We must be near the coast, near Cairns. I don't think we're over water,' said Dyer. 'This is the right heading for Cairns. I'm doing the best I can. Do we have any more flares? I need some visuals.'

There were no more flares and there was no more time. The pilots were alarmed when number one engine spluttered and died; then number two cut out. It was sooner than they'd expected. The crew heard it too. Everyone knew what was coming.

'We'll have to jump,' said Crosson. 'Leave your stations and meet at the bomb bay door. Inflate your vests. I'm going to take her up to 9000 feet while I can. Nobody jump till I give the order.'

'Arthur, get yourself back there and make sure that everyone gets out okay.'

Crosson did not trust the automatic pilot. He wanted to manually hold the ship steady while the crew prepared to jump. He reflected on the operation. What a disaster it had been. He had missed the target and the ordnance had been dropped into the sea. *Eva* was lost somewhere over north Australia and now they were going down. He may even lose his crew. All this for nothing. Crosson was mortified.

There are several exit possibilities on a B-24. An athletic crewman could jump out of the rear, or waste, windows. There was also the bottom hatch near the tail. This area was for camera mounting, but after a tight squeeze a man could exit the ship there. These options were dangerous. The chute could wrap around the tail, or, worse, you could hit the tail before you could pull the ripcord. There was also a hatch on the flight deck to the rear of the pilots and forward of the top turret. This was normally used by the flight engineer when checking that gas caps were secure or for refuelling. These hatches were ideal exits if the ship ditched into the sea. A desperate pilot could also squeeze through the sliding widows adjacent to his position. However, the best place to jump from a B-24 was through the bomb bay doors. There was plenty of room and no equipment to interdict a free fall.

Speltz grabbed the hydraulic lever on the right side of the bay and the section rolled alongside the fuselage like a roll-top desk. The moving sections were driven by large sprockets working directly on corrugated stiff inner skins. The night wind rushed through the bay, and the sound and the blackness did nothing to ease the trepidation of the men as they gathered along the catwalk.

The intercom buzzed. 'Okay, out. Everyone out,' yelled Crosson. 'See you on the ground. Good luck.'

Crosson wrestled with the controls as the men jumped into the night. 'Come on, skipper, it's time to go,' said Speltz, as he entered the flight deck. 'They've all gone. Save yourself.'

Crosson cut the throttles so *Eva* could glide. He left his seat and watched Speltz vanish through the doors. Crosson checked his harness, inflated his vest, took a fleeting look over his shoulder and dived head-first into the darkness.

As he swung like a pendulum in the night sky, he inflated his Mae West. It acted like a neck collar, making it difficult to look down. But that didn't matter, as there was nothing to see.

Like the others he was fearful about coming down in the sea. It would mean almost certain death. He braced himself for the immersion. Instead there was a thump and then blackness. Crosson did not know how long he had been unconscious — probably just minutes. He was on his back, wrapped up his chute. He could see the outline of a tree above him. He had hit it and it had hit him. His head hurt, as did his side. The life jacket had cushioned his fall or it might have been worse. There was a trickle of blood on his cheek, but his mind seemed to be functioning normally. The broken ribs were another matter. He couldn't bear to touch his side and it was difficult to breathe. It hurt as he called out in the night. There was no answer. The glow in the dark could only be the plane. It looked only a few miles away — three at most. It was burning brightly and there was the cacophony of exploding ammunition. He walked as quickly as he could towards the luminosity and the reverberations. Surely the others would do the same. With a little luck they should all meet by daybreak.

Crosson found *Eva* just before dawn, but he was not the first one there. Loy Wilson had arrived during the night and was sitting beside the wreck. He rose to his feet as he saw Crosson approaching.

'Are you the only one here?' asked Crosson.

'Yes sir, but there's something that you have to see. Workman never made it. His chute is caught on the door.'

'Oh Jesus,' said Crosson, as he saw the crumpled figure of Charles Workman still entangled in his harness, with his chute's shroud lines wrapped around the port waist latch.

Like a puppet on a string, his body had been pounded lifeless against the tail section. 'Why didn't he jump through the bomb bay doors like the rest of us?' It was a question that could never be answered. Workman was dead before the ship hit the ground.

Eva had landed belly down and had skidded for a hundred metres. The area was level with some brush and long grass. Crosson at first thought that they might have made it without jumping, but then he saw that the front section of the ship had caught fire and was totally destroyed. The port and starboard wings were intact, as was the external rear fuselage. Fire had raced through the inside of the ship. The rear gun turret had been torn from the ship and rested a few metres to the rear. There was a debris field and the occasional snap of exploding ammunition.

'There's something else,' said Wilson. 'I think that there's someone still inside.'

The two men walked to the port waist window. The fires had subsided, but inside the area was still smoldering and smokey. It was too hot to go inside, and they had no wish to do so. They gazed through the opening. In the rear of the tail section were human remains; it was a sight they would never forget.

'Oh Christ! Oh Jesus! What happened?' exclaimed Crosson. 'I thought that everyone was out. Why didn't he jump? Why didn't he jump with the rest of us? He didn't have a chance. Who do you think it is?'

'I can't be sure,' said Wilson, 'but I think it's Ed McKeon. I don't remember seeing him jump.'

Soon it was daylight and Crosson pondered the situation. No doubt the others would turn up soon. The smoke from the fire was still omnipresent — a beacon in the sky.

'We'll wait until sundown for the others. They should be here by then.'

Crosson believed that the distance between the first jump and the last was around ten miles — no more than a few hours walk. The two men waited beside the wreck. The day was long and the weather hot. By 1500 hours it was becoming doubtful whether any other crew members would return to the plane.

'They should be here by now,' said Wilson. 'Maybe they didn't make it, or maybe they've been found by a farmer or something. They could have followed a trail and walked out of this place.'

Crosson knew that a decision had to be made. He was in pain, there was no food or water and he was already feeling the pangs of thirst. There had to be a homestead close by. He could report the matter to the authorities and organise a search for the others. A search party could return to the plane and take care of the dead crew member. Another day here could make a difference. They needed their strength. So at 1800 hours on 2 December 1942, Crosson and Wilson left the *Little Eva* and headed west.

Twenty hours earlier and three hundred miles to the north-east, the first ships of the 90th Bomb Group were returning to Iron Range. It was not a good night for celestial shots and the navigators had to depend on dead reckoning. It was a bleak, dark and stormy night. Rogers, leading the 319th, had turned on his landing lights for the other ships to follow him in. This was a good idea if Rogers was able to find the base. By 2200 there was some concern. Maybe they had overflown the base, or maybe they were off course.

'There's the light,' said Rogers' navigator. 'At two o'clock … it's the searchlight from the base.'

Rogers commenced his run at 1000 feet. He had difficulty in lowering the nose wheel due to flak damage. When taxiing after landing, Rogers had to feather his engines, as his idling lever had been severed by the Japanese Zeros. The other squadrons also had difficulty in finding the base, but by 0130 the ships of the 320th, the 400th and the 321st were on the ground — all but one.

Walter Higgins had landed *Cow Town's Revenge* at 2350. Jim McMurria had arrived a few minutes before. The mission had been a modest success and no crews had been lost in action.

'Where's Fats?' asked Higgins during debriefing. 'Where's Norm Crosson?'

'We don't know,' said McMurria. 'He must still be aloft or maybe he's gone down.'

It was shortly after 2400 when the tower notified Colonel Rogers that a mayday had been received from a B-24, presumably Lieutenant Crosson's ship; the aircraft had been caught in a storm and the navigator was seeking a bearing position; it was apparently lost somewhere near the base; the situation had been desperate, as the ship's fuel was due to run out within two hours.

Frank Walden knew that the wet was coming. This meant that much of the property would be inaccessible and it was necessary to check fences and recover stray stock while the weather allowed. He had all but forgotten about the night, twelve days earlier, when he'd heard the strange aircraft noises. It was 4 o'clock in the afternoon and it was still hot. Frank was rounding up some horses with two Aboriginal stockmen; the dogs were at the horses' heels. Frank decided to put the livestock in the temporary stockyard that they had built near Pelican Waterhole on Gin Arm Creek.

At first he thought it might have been a snake when his horse, Firebolt, reined back. The dogs began barking. 'Look over there, Boss,' said one of the stockmen. Frank gazed in the direction of a tree on the far side of the creek. Two men were sitting side by side, and both began to rise. He wondered who they could be. They certainly weren't locals. Perhaps they were Japs. Frank lamented the fact that he had left his rifle back at Escott. He used it to dispatch injured stock or troublesome predators. Frank was pleased that there was a hundred yards of water between the two groups. There was further comfort when one of the men called out in a loud voice, 'Over here. Over here. We're Americans. We're American flyers. Our plane went down. We're lost.'

Frank could hear the unmistakable accents. Both men were waving and shouting in unison. They walked to the edge of the creek as if to begin crossing it.

'Stay where you are,' said Frank. 'I'll send one of the boys over to get you.'

He told one of his men to go to the crossing upstream and guide the men across the creek.

Minutes later the two groups met. 'Thank God you found us,' said the taller man. 'I'm Norman Crosson. I am a lieutenant with the 90th Bomb Group. This is Staff Sergeant Wilson. We've been lost for days. We were beginning to think that we wouldn't make it. Have you found any of the others yet?'

Frank was surprised at the state of the men. They were malnourished and badly burned by the sun and their clothes were torn. Both the men were covered in scratches, and Crosson's feet were so badly lacerated that he could hardly walk.

'Can you blokes get on a horse? We'll get you back to the house.' Frank told one of his men, George, to ride back to the homestead. 'Tell the Missus what's happened. Tell her we're on our way.'

The Americans had seldom experienced such care and kindness. Crosson grimaced as Ellen started to cut away his issue socks that had become embedded in his skin. Once removed, the socks were hung on a nail on the kitchen wall.

Wilson had his feet in a bucket of hot water. Their thirsts quenched, the two enjoyed some beverages; there was no coffee, but tea had never tasted so good. The whole property was energised by the event. Station life can be dull and routine, and the arrival of the two 'Yanks' became a focal point of interest. Frank's three sons, Edward, Roy and Francis, had returned from the paddocks once they heard the news. Staff and station hands gathered around the house. Those inside heard the first account of a remarkable odyssey.

Crosson and Wilson had decided to trace the route of *Eva's* descent in an effort to find the other crew members. Late on the first day they had come across the Cherrapunya waterholes and a dry creek bed where they spent the night. Late on December 4th, they found a small creek with salt water and believed that they were nearing the sea; they thought that it must be the Coral Sea, but it was the Gulf of Carpentaria. There were no beaches and no sign of life. After struggling for four days through mudflats and mosquito-infested swamps, they decided to turn back inland. The decision to turn east saved their lives. Food was scarce and they survived on mud grubs and a lizard Wilson had killed; it was okay if you swallowed quickly. For two days they had no water. On December 12th, they returned to the same waterholes they had encountered nine days earlier. Crosson had found what he believed to be a cattle trail, and the men agreed to follow it for as long as possible. It led to an old abandoned stockyard at Gin Arm Creek. The men were contemplating whether to attempt to cross the river, but decided to wait in the hope that someone would come along. By the time Frank Walden arrived, the men had all but given up hope.

Frank brought two large metal tubs in for the men to enjoy a hot bath. Despite their ordeal, the men talked late into the night. 'If you guys hadn't come along, we were goners,' said Crosson. 'We had no idea where we were. We expected to find help quickly.' They couldn't believe the heat. Or the mosquitoes. At night they'd covered themselves in mud to avoid being bitten.

All Crosson had eaten in three days was a few crabs. He couldn't stomach the snakes and grubs. He told Frank that he used to be called 'Fats'. But not any more: 'I must have lost fifty pounds.'

'Anything you blokes want, just ask,' said Frank.

'Do you have any Chesterfields,' asked Wilson. 'Do you have any cigarettes?'

'Sure,' said Frank. 'I've got tobacco.'

The men watched as Frank expertly rolled two cigarettes with tobacco from a leather pouch. Wilson was the first to indulge. It was a strong brand of tobacco, but the coughs did not distract from the moment.

'Try one, pal,' he said to Crosson. 'They're a little rough, but they're okay.'

As the men closed their eyes and inhaled, Ellen prepared their first cooked meal for twelve days.

'I never thought that I'd eat under a light again,' said Crosson.

'I never thought that I'd sleep under a roof again,' said Wilson.

Frank told his son Eddie to get a horse and ride to Burketown to tell the police what had happened. He also told him to call in at Iluka on the way, to alert the soldiers stationed there. The message was that a plane might have gone down near Moonlight Creek, on Marless Station.

As Eddie Walden rode into the night, for the first time in days Crosson did not think about death.

CHAPTER FOUR

'They'll be in big trouble'

THE Burketown Police Station was established in 1892. It was one of the oldest and most isolated in the state. Named after the ill-fated explorer Robert O'Hara Burke, the town is situated in the north-west of Queensland on the Albert River. It was originally built in 1862 as a supply centre for distant cattle stations. The town was resilient, as were the one hundred or more inhabitants. It had been levelled by a cyclone, threatened by a tidal wave, and in 1942 some of the older residents could remember when the town had been ravaged by the Gulf Fever plague. Most Australians knew nothing about this outback town. Accessibility was dependent on the season and the conditions. Most of those who visited Burketown believed that it reflected character and radiated a simple sincerity.

Sergeant Heinrich Nuss was not accustomed to anyone knocking on the front door of the police station at such an hour. In fact, few people knocked on the front door at any hour. It was a quiet station in a quiet district. Nuss looked at the wall clock — it was a little after 10.00 pm. The knocks became more frequent and louder. Then came a voice: 'Open up — open the door'.

Thirty-eight-year-old Nuss had only recently been posted to Burketown. A former farmer, he was an experienced officer who had served in many distant rural areas, including Thursday Island, Herberton, Forsayth and Palmwoods. Sworn in at Brisbane in August 1928, Nuss had served the force in the capacity of constable for fourteen years. In June 1942 he was awarded the rank of Sergeant 2/c. Burketown was a new phase in his career and a new life for his family. He was diminutive, reserved and modestly competent. He seldom answered to his given name of Heinrich — even less so during the war. He much preferred 'Harry'.

When Nuss cautiously opened the front door to the station verandah on that night in December 1942, he could never have imagined the events that would follow. The nervous policeman was relieved when he recognised the man as being Edward Walden, one of three brothers from Escott Station situated about ten miles from the town.

'There's an American plane that's crashed in the bush,' exclaimed Walden. 'Dad found two Yanks on the property this afternoon. One of them's the pilot. He says that they ran out of fuel and crashed about two weeks ago. It's a big bomber — a Liberator, I think. Dad reckons that it must have come down near Moonlight Creek. I told the soldiers at Iluka Station on my way here. Green, the officer, is on his way. He's bringing men for a search. The Yank says that there could still be six men lost in the bush.'

Nuss was surprised. What was an American plane doing out here? The nearest American base he knew about was at Cloncurry. Walden told him that the pilot's name was Crosson and that the aircraft had become lost during a storm. He'd been heading for their base at Iron Range, somewhere on the North Queensland coast.

Nuss suggested that Walden remain at the station so he could take notes. Lieutenant Green arrived within the hour and after a brief discussion he and Nuss agreed that a search should be undertaken as soon as possible.

On the morning of 15 December 1942 Burketown was a hive of

activity. Nuss had telegraphed his superior, Inspector Galligan, at Cloncurry about the events and to inform him that preparations were being made for an immediate search. There was no need to telegraph events throughout the Burketown district, because word of the crash and the impending search had spread like a summer bushfire.

Lieutenant Green had brought seven soldiers from 'C' Company of the Northern Australian Observer Unit with him. The other two Walden brothers arrived with horses and supplies. Two locals, Robert MacIntyre and Phil Jackson from Yarrum Station, who knew the area well were there at first light. There were others as well, locals and stockmen, thirty-five men in all, including six Aboriginals who were familiar with the area.

That same morning, Nuss was told that another search party from Gregory Downs was being formed; it was being organised by Geoffrey Colless, from Almora Station. Although the town had a police station that was also within the Cloncurry District, the search was a civilian affair without any official status. Colless sent word that his party would leave Gregory Downs and rendezvous with the Burketown party at Gum Hole, Marless Station. In a move that would later cause consternation with senior police, Nuss decided not to lead the search. His reasons may have concerned his unfamiliarity with the area. He had been in the Burketown district for only five months. Green had also told him that he had reported the matter to the RAAF Headquarters in Townsville; there was sure to be some response from them and from the police in Cloncurry. Perhaps the most important factor in his decision was the fact that the two Americans were due to arrive in the town around noon. Nuss wanted to question them and learn more about the crash. Green had also told him that he would carry a wireless set and could regularly inform him about the progress of the search. Nuss would stay in Burketown. He delegated the control of the search to his constable.

Roy Thomas Marsh had always wanted to be posted to a bush

station. Sworn-in at Brisbane on 11 June 1940, 29-year-old Marsh had arrived at Burketown a year before Nuss. In the short time that he been in the district Marsh had become a familiar figure in the town and in mounted patrols to neighbouring homesteads, usually with the Aboriginal tracker Norman.

The outbreak of war in September 1939 placed extreme pressure on the Queensland Police Force. The Commissioner of Police, Mr C. J. Carroll, was required to work in complete cooperation with the Department of Defence to provide for the protection of not only the civilian population but also public buildings and communications. The Queensland Police Department endured the extra responsibility of enforcing and administrating Commonwealth laws. Carroll immediately requested a major increase in recruiting. Annual leave for all officers was cancelled and the state government agreed to enrol an extra fifty men. Police pensioners were recalled, and chosen auxiliaries were sworn in for select duties, most notably facility and property security. To ensure that adequate police numbers were maintained during the war, the Commonwealth government directed that the members of the force be exempted from military service.

The police may have been exempt from enlistment in the armed forces, but that did not stop many members from resigning, forfeiting their privileges and leaving the security of the Force to join the newly formed 2nd AIF Divisions.

In 1939 there were 1433 members of the Queensland Police Force, with the majority of them being in the cities and major towns.

Commissioner Carroll was aware of the constant demand for police in northern and country districts. As a consequence, he gave a virtually unconditional preference to new recruits … *who were 'expert horsemen and bushmen'.*

Men like Harry Nuss received belated promotions by volunteering to serve in the bush and men like Roy Marsh were encouraged to serve in outback stations. Their motives did not concern an exuberant rate of pay. Like the members of the armed forces, police were paid a peppercorn wage. When Marsh became a constable at Burketown in 1941 he was paid £269 per year. In 1925 he would have received £300 per year. The depression had cut deep. In 1942, Harry Nuss ran the Burketown Police Station for £304 per year. But serving in the bush was different from serving in the cities. Bush skills, physical fitness and a capacity for resilience were valued as highly as initiative, intelligence and ambition.

A wartime *Police Bulletin* describes a typical country policeman's disposition and duties:

He is usually an unassuming sort of chap. He paces round the streets or stands quietly at the back of the hall during the hospital benefit concert. Sometime he makes a leisurely tour of the district, gathering statistics and drinking tea at farmsteads. He attends race meetings, picks up drunks and keeps order at the local picture-show. When the occasion demands it he carries bad news, searches for lost children, eliminates diseased animals, rescues kittens, watches the trains go out, sees that nobody drives a horse with sore shoulders and manages to shave regularly and present an unruffled appearance.

The typical country policeman was also an office-bound clerk writing copious reports to the District Inspector. The duties were indeed many, varied and extraneous. However, no amount of training could relate to the desperate situation that now confronted the two-man station at Burketown.

Nuss knew that the most important thing was to find the plane. If the men were not there, there was a chance they might have left a message on the plane or around it. Nuss told Marsh to look carefully and not to let anyone touch anything. Better still, Marsh was to put a guard around the plane.

'If no one's there and they're still alive, Christ knows where they'll be,' said Nuss. 'See if Norman can pick up any tracks and let me know what's going on so I can tell Cloncurry. If there are any bodies around, you'd better bury them, but make sure there's no suspicious circumstances. The soldiers have got a wireless, so keep in touch. Roy, just keep control of this mob. There's too many of them. Jesus, some of them are even carrying bells, in case they get lost. You have got to take charge; don't let it get out of hand. I'm going to see if I can get a Flying Doctor's plane from Cloncurry to help with the search.'

Just after 10.00 am on December 15th, Marsh, with thirty-five mounted soldiers, station hands, volunteers, Aboriginals and an extra fifteen horses, left Burketown for Gum Hole at Marless Station. Frank Walden had told police that that was the area he believed contained the crash site. Standing on the front verandah of the station, Harry Nuss watched the mob disappear from view. The scene did not inspire confidence. It looked more like a rabble than a search party and he was anything but optimistic. It had been nearly two weeks since the crash and the plane had come down in a dangerous, merciless area. The weather was hot and the trail cold.

Crosson and Wilson had spent the night in two makeshift bunks on the homestead's verandah. They talked well into the night, too excited to sleep.

They had barely awoken when the soldiers arrived to take them to Burketown.

'God bless you both,' said Crosson to Frank and Ellen as he walked towards the vehicle. 'Thank you for saving my life,' said Wilson. 'I'll never forget you.'

Crosson was about to enter the vehicle when he stopped and walked back towards Ellen. He reached for his shoulder lapel and removed his wings. He kissed Ellen on the cheek and placed the wings in her hand. 'I think that these will be a better keepsake than those old socks,' he said.

As the vehicle left through the main gate of the property, Ellen continued to wave with one hand and wipe the tears from her eyes with the other.

Nuss had received word of the imminent arrival of the two American airmen. Lieutenant Stan Chapman from 'C' Company at Iluka had been instructed to pick up Crosson and Wilson from Escott Station. At 12.30 pm on December 15th, the vehicle arrived at Burketown. Nuss and a curious crowd were there to welcome the Americans, who were to be admitted to the town's spartan, though utilitarian, four-bed hospital.

Nuss was shocked at the condition of the men. They were in a sorry state: frail, undernourished and crimson from the sun. Their limbs were lacerated and the taller of the two could barely walk; his feet were swollen and bandaged.

The initial meeting between Nuss and the Americans took only minutes. Nuss told the men that they would talk later. 'You have to find those men. I'm sure that they're still alive,' said Crosson. 'If you get me a plane I think that I can find them.'

Medical services in Australia's desolate north had always been a problem. Many towns and isolated homesteads lacked even rudimentary services. No one was more aware of the problems than Presbyterian minister and social visionary the Reverend John Flynn. Born in 1880, as a young minister Flynn was placed in charge of a small nursing home in the outback town of Oodnatta. He became deeply concerned about the lack of medical resources in the outback and as a result formed a series of nursing hostels in outback areas. He also saw the potential of using aviation for a more effective service. The problem of communication still prevailed. Flynn knew that there could be no aerial services without a radio that could work without electricity. Adelaide engineer Alf Traeger developed a remarkable and simple device called the pedal wireless, which consisted of bicycle pedals and a generator. Traeger believed that a seated operator could generate 20 watts at a pressure of 300 to 400 volts. This was sufficient to send a Morse signal.

By 1928, public subscriptions, donations and a Commonwealth Government grant enabled Flynn to form the Australian Inland Mission Aerial Medical Service (AIMAMS) based at Cloncurry. The AIMAMS chartered aircraft from the recently formed bush airline Queensland and Northern Territory Aerial Service, based in Longreach. The aviation industry was soon calling the airline 'Qantas'. In its first year the 'flying doctors' flew 18 000 miles and tendered to 225 patients. Qantas charged the fledgling service a modest fee, which included an aviation mechanic permanently stationed at the Cloncurry depot.

It was shortly after 10.00 am on Saturday, three days later, when Nuss heard the drone of an aircraft engine. Air traffic in the skies over Burketown was infrequent and never failed to stimulate the interest of the town's citizens. The weekly Airlines of Australia commercial flight was a routine affair, but that was not due until Wednesday.

As Nuss walked out of the Police Station he gazed into the sky and soon saw that it was a Flying Doctor DH 83 Fox Moth — a twin-seat bi-plane used by the Flying Doctor service in conjunction with the larger De Haviland type. He had seen both in service during his years as a constable at the remote Forsayth station.

The Moth circled the town and the pilot waved to the crowd and then pointed to the town centre, indicating that the pilot was preparing to land in the main street. Nuss shouted for the crowd to clear the area and to stand back. Landings such as this were not without an element of danger, but to the flying doctors used to landing in rough bush strips, it was virtually routine.

Everyone watched as the aircraft approached the town centre and landed without mishap. As the crowd flocked to the now stationary Moth, Nuss greeted the pilot, Ian Hosie. Soon both men were at the station looking over a map of the area.

'We think that the plane went down near here,' said Nuss as he pointed to Moonlight Creek.

Hosie told Nuss that he could devote two days to the search but would then have to return to Cloncurry. He would take off in the afternoon and fly over the area. His first priority was locating the Liberator and any sign of the men. If he came across the Marsh party he would try and contact them, although this was easier said than done. Without radio contact, the only way he could get a message to a ground party was by placing a hand-written note in a metal canister and throwing it from the aircraft.

Hosie filled up his petrol tanks, had a cup of tea and a sandwich, and after some cheers from the folk of Burketown flew off in the direction of the assumed crash site — fifty miles north-west of the town.

No sooner had the Moth disappeared over the horizon than a rider arrived at the police station and began calling for the police sergeant. It was the Aboriginal tracker, Norman, who had left with the search party three days earlier. Norman carried a written report from Marsh.

Arrived at Gum Hole at 10.00 am on Wednesday. We split into three groups and made three different camps. Green and three of his men and tracker Norman accompanied Frank Walden to the waterhole where the American pilot said was only about five miles from where the plane had crashed. We arrived at this waterhole on Friday the 18th. We searched for the plane that afternoon and again on Saturday with negative results. The bush is very thick in this area. It is full of Ti scrub. It is impossible to see more than fifty yards ahead. We will keep searching. It is hard to keep order here. The soldiers will only take orders from Green. The Waldens, MacIntyre and Jackson are off looking somewhere. Geoff Colless has arrived with more men. There are others as well. I don't know a lot of them. Is there any news of the Doctor's plane? We need more horses.

'Why can't they report by wireless?' Nuss asked Norman. 'The one that the soldiers took with them.'

'It's buggered,' said Norman. 'A horse rolled over on it. A lot of horses are knocked up.'

Nuss told Norman to return to the search party and to tell Marsh to keep in touch and that a Flying Doctor's plane was assisting in the search. Nuss visited the Americans in the hospital to tell them of developments. Crosson asked Nuss to tell his people to recover the bombsight from the plane, as it was 'top secret' and had to be returned to the proper authorities.

Nuss returned to the hospital later that night to let the Americans know that Hosie had located the wrecked aircraft and also six parachutes. He had not, however, located any of the search parties. Tomorrow he would return to the area to try and get word to the ground party as to the crash location.

Nuss telegraphed Cloncurry with news of this first positive development: 'Hosie located plane today. Six parachutes also located. Ground parties to be directed to the area tomorrow. We need more horses.'

Hosie told Nuss that the Liberator was in thick scrub country on Marless Station. The area was heavily timbered and he had not seen any sign of survivors and no one from the Marsh group. Two of the parachutes were in one area and four were a few miles away.

All involved with the search dreaded the gathering of dark clouds and the sprinkling of rain. The wet season in the Gulf can transform dry wasteland into inland lakes and boggy swamps. Creeks overflow their banks and rivers flood the low areas. Communities can become isolated and travellers imperiled. The season usually occupies the late summer months. The hand of fate had dealt the Americans aviators another cruel blow. The wet season started early that year — in mid-December.

The Marsh group had heard the Moth as it circled the area. Marsh's later account of the group's attempts to contact the aircraft suggests that looking for the lost aviators was not the only challenge confronting the search parties:

We made for the sound of the plane. But he flew further to the west and did not stay to direct us to the crash spot. We searched where he appeared to dive but could not locate anything. We then returned to the camp thinking that he may have dropped a message with the directions to the plane, but he never went near the camp. We left to search again but had only gone about half a mile when we heard the plane again so we returned to the camp thinking that he may have gave us directions, but he apparently did not see the camp, as there was another camp about two and a half miles from us and he probably mistook them for us, as we were the ones he was to drop messages to.

Hosie returned to the area the following day and finally made contact with the party led by Robert MacIntyre. Hosie directed the party to the crashed aircraft, only ten miles away. Lieutenant Green arrived in the MacIntyre camp and was told the news. Some hours later Marsh was surprised when Green arrived to tell of the sighting and that his soldiers had also found four parachutes. Marsh immediately made arrangements to move camp. He signalled the other searchers with a flare.

On the morning of December 21st, the sixth day of the search, Marsh and eighteen men left camp to resume the search. Marsh later reported:

We searched in the direction given by the pilot for about two and a half miles but could not find any trace of the plane; apparently we did not go far enough, but we searched all day until 4 pm and then returned to the camp for dinner. During the day some very heavy rain fell and the sky was overcast all day. The country became very boggy.

The next development was a result of what was later reported as being the consequences … 'of not having an active leader to exercise authority'.

Marsh later reported:

… the next morning some of the men decided to abandon the search, because of the weather. Green decided that we continue the search with a party that would have consisted of ten white men and tracker Norman, but when Green saw the others getting ready to leave he packed up and went too; everyone left with the exception of MacIntyre, Jackson and the Waldens, but they left the next morning. Tracker Norman and I returned to where the parachutes were with the pack horse. It appeared useless only two of us continuing the search. We experienced some difficulty in getting out of the country as it was very boggy after the rain. All the creeks and gullies were running. We arrived at Burketown at 12.30 pm on December 24.

Nuss knew that the search had been abandoned well before Marsh and Norman arrived. Local men had began returning to the town earlier in the day. It was Lieutenant Green who told him that the area was too boggy for the horses. 'Twenty horses are knocked up,' he said. 'It's too wet out there. I'm taking my men back to Iluka until the weather eases.'

When Marsh returned and began carrying the parachutes into the station, he was confronted by Nuss. 'Christ, Roy! Couldn't you have stayed out there a little longer and found the plane. Hosie said it was only a few miles away. There's men still missing; they could still be waiting near the plane.'

'It's too wet and muddy,' said Marsh. 'We couldn't find the plane, only the parachutes. Everybody shot through. It was only me and Norman. We only had three horses left. What could we do? We can go out again later.'

Harry Nuss knew that this incident was quickly becoming a major issue with police and the military. It was just his luck that the wrecked

Liberator lay within the boundaries of his district. He cursed the fact that it was now his responsibility.

'Carroll in Brisbane knows about this now,' said Nuss. 'The Americans want the plane found and Cloncurry have asked for a report. What am I going to tell them? We couldn't find the Americans — we couldn't even find the bloody plane!' He paused. 'Anyway it's not over yet. I've just got a telegram from Galligan in Cloncurry — Bob Hagarty is on his way from Gregory Downs.'

The Gregory Downs Station was at the eastern apex of the Cloncurry Police District. It was a small town, even older than Burketown, and was yet another supply centre for the many distant properties in the region. Formerly under the control of Burketown Police, the town received its own police presence in 1932 when a new station was built. Since 1937, the station had been administered by Robert Phillip Hagarty. Sworn into the force on 17 October 1932, Hagarty began his service in Mackay and Windorah.

By 1942, the 33-year-old constable had become an integral part of the country community and was much admired and respected. Hagarty lived in the small station with his wife, Alice, and their two young children, Pat and Mary.

Hagarty's value to the force was considerable. His skills were not just confined to horsemanship; unlike all of his city colleagues and most white men, he could live off the land. During a dry spell he could find water in the trunks of trees and shrubs. For food he could dine on swamp turtles and mussels. The bush was a familiar domain and it was possible to survive in it, providing you knew where to look and what to do. Hagarty and Herb Lewis from Springsure were considered the two best bushmen in the Queensland Police Force.

Hagarty had heard of the crash and that a search was under way. He was also aware of the party being formed by Geoff Colless and had advised the group as to the best route to Burketown. He had wondered how Nuss and Marsh were coping with the incident. It was a Burketown problem and he would observe with interest. However, he became officially involved with the Liberator of Moonlight Creek on Monday, 18 December 1942. It was 5.50 pm when a telegram was delivered to the station:

> You are to proceed to Burketown at the earliest and render all possible assistance in search operation for missing American airmen … Galligan.

It was not often that a country constable would receive an urgent telegram from the district inspector. Visits were even less frequent. For the entire year of 1941 Inspector Galligan did not walk into the Gregory Downs Police Station. It was a massive district — half the size of Great Britain — and there were no phone lines and no radio. Typical communication was by written reports conveyed by the post office. It was not an express service; reports from Gregory Downs could take up to three weeks to be received at Cloncurry.

Hagarty was an isolated policeman working in an insulated community. His regular contact with the Police Department occurred fortnightly when he collected his wages from the post office. There were few reasons to spend his pay. Townsfolk and property owners overwhelmed his family with fresh meat, fruit and vegetables. The kitchen and stove access at the rear of the police station were well utilised through regular cooking and the making of bread, the equal of any in the town. The station also had a dining verandah, two living rooms and a small office. The 1000-gallon rainwater tank never ran dry during the summer months. The station had no lock-up, but Hagarty had been known to handcuff troublemakers to a tree. He also carried a pair of leg irons that he would not hesitate to use on any offender, black or white. Hagarty did not concern himself with the formalities of the various regulation police manuals. His was a different world from that of the city police. His attire was more suitable to his environment than to the parade ground and he never lost any sleep over possessing non-standard weapons.

Those Queensland Police who were issued rifles invariably used the standard Lee-Enfield .303 carbine. Hagarty found the weapon too heavy and cumbersome, particularly when he was on horseback. Instead he used an old Martini-Enfield .303, Mark 1, which was one of the weapons the Australian forces used in the Boer War.

In 1942, this single-shot weapon was already over forty years old. Hagarty preferred it because it was lighter and shorter than the Lee-Enfield and he found that he could shoot it with one hand while mounted. In addition, the weapon had a lesser recoil and the discharge did not seem to spook his mount as much. Hagarty undoubtedly procured this weapon from a Boer War surplus sale, but the circumstances that allowed him to obtain a Luger hand gun will never be known. When undertaking a mounted patrol Hagarty always used these weapons, as well as a long-bladed hunting knife that he wore in a sheath on his waist. Resilient, resolute and resourceful, Bob Hagarty was as tough as nails.

At the rear of the station was a small hut that provided accommodation for the Aboriginals employed by the police. In the official vernacular, the hut was to be occupied by the 'Aboriginal tracker and his gin'.

In a 'White Australia' culture the Indigenous people were not considered socially desirable; in fact they were not considered at all. They were not counted in any census and had few civil rights. Since the arrival of the Europeans, the independent, culturally conscious Aboriginal population had become a poverty-stricken, dependent and brutally oppressed minority. Most lived in harsh outback areas or in segregated reserves. Generations of Australians had been indoctrinated to ignore them. They were 'Abos', 'Blackfellas' or 'Boongs', relevant to the past but increasingly irrelevant to the present.

Bob Hagarty had no such preconceptions. In his world the

Aboriginals enjoyed a more important status, particularly the trackers. He referred to them as 'my colleagues', and when compiling reports he referred to them by name and seldom mentioned their race.

Since the last decades of the nineteenth century black trackers had provided useful service to the Queensland Police Force, but like the horse their days were numbered. In 1900 there were 120 trackers in the force; by 1939 there were only 39. Most trackers were recruited locally, and a recommendation sent to the district inspector and then to Brisbane. Once approved, the Aboriginal was employed by the Queensland Police Department. He was given a blue uniform with a red stripe down the side of the trousers. He earned the princely sum of £1 per week, plus 'tucker'. It was a poor wage even by police standards. The department responded to criticism by calling the pay 'a retainer'. Many Aboriginals left the service without warning or explanation, never to return. Many were tempted north to the big cattle stations, where a competent black stockman could earn as much as £7 per week.

'They do not need a scent or a track to pick up a trail. They can even follow a trail at night,' said the police media. The trackers were indeed skilled at finding lost souls, or pursuing felons. The legendary Snowy Fraser once tracked a safe-blower along a bitumen road, until he found the loot under a railway bridge. Other duties for the trackers were more mundane — domestic chores, errands, cutting the grass, feeding the horses and clearing away rubbish. The 14 ft x 12 ft tracker shed at the rear of the Gregory Downs Police Station was built in 1939. It provided no more comforts than a horse would enjoy. In 1942 it was occupied by an Aboriginal called Archie. Hagarty respected Archie for his skills, often turning a blind eye when Archie felt the need to go back and visit his country. He received pay and lodgings, except when he went 'walkabout'.

Within minutes of receiving the Galligan telegram, Hagarty instructed Archie to prepare to travel to Burketown. It was a major journey — 75 miles on horseback over primitive roads. And now that steady rain was falling, the roads were virtually unusable.

Two horses, Tiger and Blossom, and two pack animals would make the journey. On the afternoon of December 21st, Bob Hagarty pulled on his knee-length boots, gathered his weapons and said goodbye to Alice and the children. Archie waited with the horses and soon the two men were gone. The journey normally took about two and a half days, but this time, due to the wet, it would take over three.

When Hagarty and Archie walked through the front door of the Burketown Police Station at 10.00 pm on December 24th, it may have been the Christmas spirit that consoled them when Nuss told them that the search had been called off. It had been a long and arduous ride and it appeared that it had been for nothing. Nuss invited the men to spend Christmas in Burketown, which was better than spending it in the bush. Hagarty would stay in the station and Archie in the tracker's hut.

Hagarty was no stranger to Burketown. He and Roy Marsh had worked together on joint stock patrols and had been in the Moonlight Creek and Browns Creek areas on two occasions. He knew the area and was surprised that searchers had been unable to locate the plane. He would have liked to talk to Crosson and Wilson, but they had flown to Cairns some days before.

The official search may have been curtailed, but many other attempts were made to find the men. Most searches, large or small, were impromptu and disorganised. Homesteaders and Aboriginals wandered through the bush looking for anything that might provide a clue as to the whereabouts of the men. On Christmas Day, twenty-three days after the crash, four Aboriginals from the Mornington Island mission station found the tracks of four men in the coastal vicinity of Rainbow Creek. The group immediately returned to the mission and informed the superintendent. The closest property was Corinda Station. The manager, George Burns, was contacted by pedal wireless and was asked to meet with the Aboriginals who had found the tracks. The group soon found irrefutable proof that a group of men, undoubtedly white, had recently camped in the area. The carcass of a bird was found near an open fire site and twenty yards away an alert searcher found four empty cartridge shells. Burns knew that it could only be the Americans. The tracks were followed until they petered out near Cliffdale Creek. The discovery of a leather flying-jacket floating in the creek removed any doubts. It was retrieved and upon inspection the name 'J. B. Hilton' was found stamped on the collar.

Nuss could barely control his excitement after hearing the news. He related the information to Hagarty, including the fact that Burns thought that the tracks could be eight to ten days old.

Hagarty was bewildered. 'They must be heading north. What in God's name are they doing? Where are they going? There's nothing there. We'd better find them soon, otherwise they'll be in big trouble.'

John Patrick Galligan was a career police officer. In December 1942 he was fifty-seven years old and had been in the force for thirty-five years. The former labourer had served mostly in rural and isolated stations. Few would have heard of Avondale, Imbil, Chillagoe and Kolan. Galligan had served in all of these remote posts and other less spartan centres like Beaudesert, Maryborough and Cairns.

When John Galligan reported for his first day of duty in Bundaberg on 11 November 1907, he was a 21-year-old Constable. Thirty-three years later Galligan, with his wife and six children, was posted to Cloncurry as Inspector. He was in charge of the entire Cloncurry District.

John Galligan was winding down his career as a policeman. Like all members he was required to retire on his sixtieth birthday — 9 September 1945. He wanted to complete his career in a positive fashion and leave the force with his reputation assured.

The American Liberator lying near Moonlight Creek was

becoming a national incident and perhaps the last major one of his career. The matter had reached the attention of Commissioner Carroll in Brisbane, who was reporting directly to the American authorities. The facts had now reached the press and the department was under pressure. Everyone wanted the Americans found. Galligan had told Carroll that a major search was under way. On December 27th, he received a telegram from Nuss that the search had been discontinued. Nuss did not have to wait long for a reply:

Position unsatisfactory. Please furnish full report why search discontinued when Police Party in locality of plane.

Galligan's feelings on the matter were obvious in his report to Carroll:

To me it appears that Sergeant Nuss did not appreciate the importance of the search, that the lives of six men were at stake, that two men who had escaped had existed for a period of eleven days, and that if the search was properly organised and carried out there was the possibility of some of them being found alive. Instead of going out himself and exercising control and giving directions he left the matter for a junior constable. I did not receive a report from Sergeant Nuss until I asked for one. The report was mostly confined to what he did rather than what happened.

Galligan had no mercy on Nuss, who had sent his report by ordinary post:

Had he been alert he could have sent it by a Flying Doctor who was in Burketown. There are men's lives at stake. I gave consideration to going to Burketown by police utility, but weather conditions were not all together favourable.

Galligan at least could relay the positive news that there was evidence that the Americans had been in a known area and the search was to be resumed. The Cloncurry inspector concluded his report:

> A large search party is no longer desirable. The country is vast and uninhabited. It is a savage wilderness. Constables Hagarty, Marsh, with police trackers, will immediately continue the search in the area of Rainbow Creek.

CHAPTER FIVE

'Even blackfellas don't come here'

B OB HAGARTY knew that the search for the American airmen was becoming a major priority with the Queensland Police Department. The finding of the tracks near Rainbow Creek by the Mornington Island Aborigines had galvanised the authorities and he knew that the search had to be resumed immediately. He had been back at Gregory Downs only a week when Galligan ordered him by radio telegram to return to Burketown. It was also obvious that there was a sense of urgency with the new search — Galligan had authorised him to requisition a vehicle if possible and if the roads were usable.

Hagarty did not need to borrow a vehicle. His old but reliable Fargo had provided solid service in the past and should be adequate for the trip to Burketown. Hagarty was to take Archie, his saddle, harness, weapons and a few essential items. Nuss could supply the rest, including the horses. At 5.00 pm on 10 January 1943, for the second time in two weeks, Hagarty left the Gregory Downs Police Station to venture north to Burketown. He would have preferred not to start so late in the day; driving in the dark on rough, wet roads was not desirable, but he did not want to waste precious hours. With Archie sitting in the front passenger seat, the loaded Fargo was soon lost in the distance.

Harry Nuss was feeling the pressure. He knew that Bob Hagarty was returning, but of more concern was the fact that Ted Wallace, a senior sergeant from Cloncurry, was also on his way. Wallace was due to arrive with a Flying Doctor's plane that was rejoining the search. Nuss knew that it was an obvious challenge to his ability to handle the affair.

Wallace arrived with pilot Fred Elphinstone at 8.00 pm on Saturday, January 9th. The forty-year-old sergeant walked from the Fox Moth and into the station. He told Nuss that there was disappointment about the way the first search had been conducted, but he was in Burketown to do what he could, and he intended to accompany Elphinstone on his search the following morning.

'Harold, this American plane business is getting big,' he told Nuss. 'Inspector Galligan would have been here instead of me but he's got to go to Mount Isa for a murder trial.'

Wallace told Nuss that there was still hope that the remaining American flyers could be found. 'I think that Bob Hagarty will get here on Monday night. He's trying to get here by motor vehicle. He's bringing his tracker. No one wants to waste any time. The Americans want some of the equipment recovered, something to do with a bombsight.'

Nuss remembered Crosson talking about this device. Wallace told him that it had to be returned to the Burketown Station as soon as possible and placed under lock and key. Galligan was to be notified at once, so he could contact the American Military at Cloncurry.

The single-engined Fox Moth left Burketown at 7.00 am the following morning. Wallace was not in the spare seat. Elphinstone did not know the country well and Nuss had sent word to Robert MacIntyre from Yarrum Station to come to Burketown and assist with the search. MacIntyre knew the area as well as anyone, but he had never seen it from above. He was both excited and nervous about his first flight in an aeroplane.

It was not just the Qantas planes that were in the skies over Burketown. For days, American heavy bombers had been seen flying in the area, obviously searching for the men. This frustrated Nuss, because the Americans never sought to coordinate their search with that of the police. Their aircraft were seen flying in all directions.

Elphinstone stayed aloft as long as possible and managed to reach the area of Horse Creek, twenty miles from Burketown, before following the coast to the Northern Territory border. MacIntyre believed that they might find some tracks on or near the coast. He estimated that they covered 150 miles. On the way back they flew inland, searching creek beds and looking for any sign of life. It was an optimistic exercise that came to nothing. It had been seventeen days since the Mornington Island group had found the tracks; rain, mud, wind and dust had long since obliterated any signs, at least from the air.

The next morning, with Wallace aboard, the aircraft resumed the search, travelling north-west from where the wreck was believed to be. The route was once again along the coast. They crossed thirty miles over the Northern Territory border. Elphinstone flew over Bundella Creek and then suddenly he saw a group of people in the distance, walking along the beach in a north-westerly direction. He motioned to Wallace and quickly dropped altitude and flew in the direction of the group. Could this be the Americans? The group quickly dispersed as if fearful. Then they stood firm and waved, presumably recognising the distinctive markings on the aircraft. Wallace tapped the shoulder of Elphinstone and shook his head. It was obvious that this was a group of Aboriginals, perhaps returning to the mission, or perhaps still searching. It didn't matter. Finding the Americans was not going to be that easy.

Wallace had asked that the Moth return to Burketown via the area where the crashed aircraft had been sighted three weeks earlier. He wanted to see the wreck from the air, but it was not to be. At 3.00 pm, the Moth landed at Burketown, the day having yielded nothing. The one thing obvious to Wallace was the sheer enormity of the search area. If the airmen were still alive, they were probably injured or exhausted, and unable to venture into the open. If they were to be found, he believed that it would only be by a land party.

Later that day the Moth commenced the two-hour return flight to Cloncurry. Wallace spent the time observing the majesty of the country below. He could see the coastline and the setting of the sun, but what he could not see was a Fargo truck, far below, motoring in the direction of Burketown.

Hagarty arrived in Burketown at 8.00 pm on January 10th. Nuss was waiting for him. Hagarty and Archie were invited to spend the night at the station — Hagarty in a spare station room and Archie in the trackers hut. Nuss had been directed to instruct Hagarty about search priorities 'When you find the plane see if anyone has left any signs or messages,' he told Hagarty. 'The bombsight has to be found and returned here, so the Yanks can pick it up. Wallace brought drawings of it and where it should be on the plane.

'Finding the plane is the important thing,' he emphasised. 'After that you're on your own, but Bob, the locals reckon the Americans are already dead. It's been nearly six weeks. They reckon you're wasting your time, but Galligan wants them found, dead or alive.' Nuss shook his head. 'Carroll in Brisbane is demanding reports. It's driving me mad. Everyone wants to get involved.'

Hagarty's strategy was to use a small search party with competent bushmen. Big parties usually ended up with searchers looking for searchers.

'I need sixteen good horses and supplies,' Hagarty told Nuss. 'I'll need a couple of pounds of flour, some tinned beef, sugar, and a couple of tins of syrup. We can get some tucker in the bush. There's plenty of strays wandering around. We'll need new mounts. I'll need a written authority from you to get horses from the homesteads. And

Harry, we need some smokes. Can you get us a few ounces of Log Cabin and some matches — the ones that come in a tin? I want to leave tomorrow afternoon. I'd like to get to Frank Walden's place before dark.'

The party consisted of Hagarty, Roy Marsh, and the trackers Archie and Norman. The extra supplies and horses were needed in case the Americans were found. There were potentially six of them. When found they would be taken to the nearest homestead or town.

Hagarty knew good horseflesh. The police stud at Springsure, where stock was bred for police department use, was a noble failure. The animals became city horses, soft and placid; this was okay for marches and parades, but in the bush a man's life depended on his mount. Bush horses were tough and spirited and Hagarty needed to choose his stock well. He knew that this was going to be a difficult journey — as tough as he had encountered. Much of the country had never been seen by a white man. The conditions were unknown as well. The land could be both parched and boggy. Like Galligan had said, it was a savage wilderness; tough and unforgiving, it favoured no one.

Hagarty had undertaken mounted stock patrols with Roy Marsh shortly after the young constable had joined the Burketown constabulary. Together, they had ridden around the Moonlight Creek and Browns Creek areas. Hagarty was familiar with the territory and had made a camp near Durriejellpa Hole fourteen months previously. He and Marsh believed that this was where they would find the American plane. Although Hosie had found the wreck from the air, it did not make it any easier to find it by ground party; the bush was so thick that in some areas you couldn't see more than twenty yards in either direction.

The policemen were glad to arrive at Escott Station. Frank and Ellen Walden were there to greet them. Homesteaders were always pleased to see mounted patrols. It gave them a sense of security and eased the feeling of isolation. Frank Walden knew that they were coming. Nuss had sent word and had requested a selection of horses be made available to the party.

Later in the evening Hagarty asked Frank to draw a diagram indicating where he believed the Liberator might be.

'Bob, surely you don't think that the Americans are still alive?' said Frank. 'It's been six weeks since the crash. Where could they be? If the tracks near Rainbow Creek belong to them, they must be up in the Gulf country, and if that's the case they're dead by now. Take my word for it.'

'You could be right, Frank,' said Hagarty. 'But they're young and fit. Perhaps some of them know something about the bush. If they can find water and food, they could be sheltering somewhere. They could have reached the coast. For all we know, they could be waiting at the plane.'

Hagarty and Marsh spent a comfortable night at Escott Station — they knew that it would be their last comfortable night for a while.

At 8.00 am, the party was ready to leave. The two policemen were in front, with Archie and Norman at the rear and a line of twelve horses in between. The party aimed to reach Beeshed Creek, about twenty-five miles away, by nightfall, Gum Hole the next night, and Durriejellpa Hole the next. From there they would begin the search for the plane.

Soon the party was gone. The most arduous and determined search ever undertaken by the Queensland Police Force had begun.

They kept to their schedule and made Gum Hole by 5.00 pm on the 13th, but the trip was already posing problems. Two days after leaving Escott, they had made fifty miles, but on January 14th they encountered dense ti-tree scrub and heavy ground; and they made only twelve miles that day. Hagarty decided to rest the animals for a day. This also allowed the men to construct a camp that would serve as a base for an all-out search for the aircraft, which the men believed must be within a ten-mile radius of their position. The group rose early on the morning of January 16th. It was hot and dry; the vast rains had gone; all that remained were the effects on the barren country.

Hagarty wanted to keep a tight grip on the search. He wanted to miss nothing. The men formed a half-circle search fan and began walking in a north-westerly direction. They were no more than two hundred yards apart — within shouting distance. For hours the men cautiously and laboriously covered the area. It was hot and it was frustrating. Hagarty knew that there were no short cuts. It was not just the plane that he wanted to find, but also any signs of the missing men.

'Hey! Over here, everyone, over here! I think I've found something.' It was Roy Marsh and the time was 11.00 am.

Hagarty galloped towards Marsh. Norman and Archie were already there. Roy pointed. There was something up ahead that had nothing to do with the Gulf country. It was man-made; it was an American bomber. The men dismounted and Hagarty began making notes in his diary for a report that he knew he would have to compile. Later he described the scene:

The plane appeared to have crashed flat on its belly, and was lying with nose pointing to the south-west. Tree trunks were touching the edges of both front and rear portions of each wing. The wings are about two feet above ground level, and under the butt of the port wing a large rubber tyre is partly visible. Fire had completely gutted the plane from the nose as far back as the rear gunner's turret, and as far out each wing as the 1st port and starboard engines.

The upper portion of the fuselage was consumed by fire to within about four feet of the rear side door. There is a large burnt and broken hole in the top of the fuselage in front of the cross section of the tail. From the outside of the 1st port and starboard engines to the tip of each wing is intact. The twin tails, and cross section of the tail is intact with the exception of the front portion of the port tail or fin, which is damaged. All the vital forward portion of the body of the plane is a mass of molten metal and glass. The rear gun turret is completely broken off, and lies about nine yards away from, and directly in line with, the rear of the plane. The turret is untouched by fire but is badly buckled.

The rear machine gun and stand has broken away from its fastenings, and lies between the turret and the after end of the plane. The gun is untouched by fire, but the barrel is slightly bent. Much live ammunition for this gun is strewn about the ground near and in the turret. Much spent ammunition is scattered round the wreck, having been seen exploding by the fierce fire which gutted the plane.

'Let's have a look for the bombsight,' said Hagarty. 'Try not to touch anything else. It should be near the pilot part of the plane. Archie and Norman, get to the front part of the plane. Yell out if you see it. It's like a camera. If you find it, call out, but don't touch …'

Hagarty's plea was cut short by a cry from Norman, 'Hey Boss, come here quick.'

Hagarty saw the outline of a silk parachute, caught on a door of the plane. Then he saw the limp and broken body of a man, still attached to the harness. The odour of decaying flesh became all too apparent. It was a grim find, but it was only the beginning. A subsequent search inside the aircraft revealed the remains of three more crewmen. Hagarty's later report left nothing to the imagination:

The charred remains of two men were found in the rear portion of the fuselage, lying side by side with heads towards the rear of the plane. Many bones of the bodies were broken and some missing. Fasteners and metal work of the parachute harness give rise to the opinion that these two men were lying down with their parachutes when the plane crashed. The remains of a third man were found near the rear door on the starboard side of the plane. Small portions of the skull, several teeth and small bones of the hand were the only portions of the body found. Burnt metal work and fasteners of parachute harness was found close to the body.

The body of a fourth man was found lying full length on the ground outside the plane. An opened parachute was attached to the body and the silk cloth was caught in the iron work near the bottom of the port rear door. The remains were clad in a faded blue full suit overalls, leather jacket, shirt and athletic singlet, boots probably size 7 and dark coloured socks. The lower left leg was broken and the right leg was broken in two places. One hand and a portion of the lower left arm was missing and so also was the major portion of the skull. In searching clothing, I saw that most of the bones of the body were broken and the body was in the last stages of liquid putre-faction. I would say that this man was about 5 ft 9 or 10 ins tall, 11 st to 12 st weight with brown hair. Of the other three bodies that were burnt in the plane and which I have already mentioned, I cannot say anything as regards their description, except that on one man of the two which were lying together was probably a big man, judging by the lower leg bones and knee cap.

After a thorough search no identification discs or other means of identifi-cation could be found.

It was getting dark and Hagarty had had enough for the day. The group returned to the base camp to ponder the next move. Hagarty was dismayed that no one had told them about bodies being in or near the aircraft. The two Americans must have known, and Harry Nuss should have known. Hagarty and his colleagues had been confronted by a ghastly scene that they had not been expecting. There was also the problem of what to do with the bodies. Hagarty found it difficult to understand why the two Americans who had arrived at the wreck soon after the crash did not bury the bodies. The ground was hard and there may have been no tools available, but the bodies could have at least been covered. He felt very sorry for the dead men. They rested in a desolate, foreign land; they were alone; they had no identity and no dignity. The day had been sullen and sombre but there was also some good news. They were no longer looking for six survivors — now there were only four.

It was almost 8.00 pm when the men arrived back at the camp.

Supplies were getting low and Hagarty knew that he would need more. He also knew that the equipment, if found, needed to be taken back to Burketown as soon as possible. The dead could be left there until a larger party could be organised from Burketown. Hagarty had a restless night. He felt sad about the Americans. He decided to bury them as soon as they returned to the site in the morning. Supper tasted good for the hungry men; the tea was even better. The pot stayed on the fire for most of the night. The smoldering fire helped drive away the mosquitoes.

'Bob, what do you think happened to the blokes at the plane?' asked Marsh. 'Why didn't they jump like the others.'

Hagarty could only speculate, but there were two likely scenarios.

'I reckon that the bloke with the parachute jumped and pulled his ripcord too early and got caught up in the door. Maybe his mates tried to untangle him, until it became too late. They could also have been too scared to jump and decided to go down with the plane, taking their chances with the crash. Poor buggers, they didn't stand a chance.'

January 17th was bright and sunny and, as always, very hot. The men left the camp at 7.00 am and this time they took an extra pack animal. Hagarty sent Norman south and west of Browns Creek and Archie north and south. They were to search for tracks of the missing men, in case they had only recently left the area. Hagarty thought this unlikely — looking for bodies was becoming the most likely scenario.

It was Marsh who found the Norden bombsight. 'Is this the bloody thing, Bob? I found it under some stuff at the front of the plane.' Hagarty took the item and held it towards the sun. It was mangled and looked incomplete, but it seemed to match the drawing that they had been given.

'That's it. That's the damn thing all the fuss is about. See if you can find any more of it. It looks like there's something missing.'

Nothing that looked as if it was part of the bombsight could be found. The area was littered with hundreds of pieces of aircraft and equipment. Hagarty took the Norden, wrapped it up in a cloth and placed it beside a tree, and continued to search the aircraft for any personnel identification. As instructed, Hagarty noted the serial number of the aircraft: Type B24D, No: 123762.

An excited Norman rode into the area, with Archie close behind.

Norman was wrapped in a large silk parachute. He told Hagarty that he had found it about a mile and a half from the plane in a south-westerly direction. Hagarty believed that it had belonged to either Crosson or Wilson and he doubted that it was connected to the other missing men. The tracker had also picked up some faint tracks near Browns Creek. They were barely visible — probably weeks old — and were heading west. Norman said that the tracks were made by men with shoe leather. Hagarty was not surprised. He was beginning to believe that the men were not in the crash area and never had been. But why were they heading north-west?

Harry Nuss had not been idle. There were plenty of people, in and out of uniform, who were prepared to tell him how to conduct the search for the American aircraft. Robert MacIntyre had suggested that he wire Cloncurry to organise a plane to search inland from the coast between Point Parker and Settlement Creek. 'That's where you'll find them Harry, I'm sure of it.' Galligan was in constant touch. His last telegram was received on January 15th: 'Any further trace of missing airmen?'

'No further trace of missing airmen,' Nuss had replied. What else could he say? As far as Nuss was concerned, there was no point in Galligan asking him every other day. If he knew something, then Galligan would be the first to know. The trouble was that Nuss knew nothing. In fact he hadn't heard from Hagarty in nearly ten days. He dreaded the implication: was the group in trouble?

Nuss was in the main street of Burketown on January 20th when he saw a horseman riding towards the police station. It was the tracker Norman. He was followed soon after by Archie, the tracker from Gregory Downs. The men were the bearers of the first good news Nuss had received since this unwelcome affair began.

Norman told him that they had found the plane and that there had been four bodies in the wreckage. He described how they had buried the men the next day, using oxygen tanks to mark the sites. He gave Nuss the remains of the Norden bombsight, still wrapped in an old cloth. There was also a note from Hagarty:

Marsh and myself waiting at the plane. Please advise if you want the plane to be guarded. We need more provisions and horses. Do you wish for the search to continue? We have found faint tracks near Browns Creek. I believe that the Americans are headed westward towards the coast.

Nuss couldn't get to the telegram office quickly enough. At last he had something positive to report to Galligan:

Re plane crash Tracker Norman arrived today. Reported party located plane Saturday. Four dead at plane. Bodies buried, police party continuing search other men. Shall guard plane. Tracker waiting reply. Advise.

Galligan replied in hours: 'Yours today continue search. No need to further guard plane.'

Norman and Archie were given fresh provisions and fresh mounts and returned to the crash site. They carried a copy of Galligan's wire to give to Hagarty.

Hagarty and Marsh had not waited at the plane for any period of time. It seemed pointless to guard the wreck, it having lain unmolested for six weeks. Hagarty decided to continue the search as far as the coast. He did not expect the boys to be back until the 23rd at the earliest, and he didn't want to waste any more time. If any of the Americans were still alive, they had to be located soon. The two policemen travelled to the Browns Creek area where Norman had found the tracks of the men. The spot was conveniently marked with a pile of sticks.

Roy Marsh was an excellent tracker. He eventually found the place where the men had crossed the creek. The tracks became fainter and then vanished. The direction was indeed west. The two men reached the coast and rode as far as the old Doomadgee Mission, but they found no further traces of the missing men. They did come across a group of Mornington Island Aboriginals who were on their way to Burketown. The mission superintendent, Reginald Braunholz, had told them to be on the lookout for any signs of the missing men, but they had seen nothing. The two men arrived back at the wreck site at noon on January 23. Marsh noted that they had travelled around fifty miles in two and a half days, and had confirmed that the Americans had indeed headed towards the coast.

Their return to the wreck had been timely. Two hours after their return, Norman and Archie arrived with provisions, fresh mounts and new orders.

The instructions from Galligan gave Hagarty the discretion to search wherever he wanted for as long as he wanted; he could even venture into the Northern Territory. He knew that if the Americans were still alive, his party represented the best chance of finding them.

At 7.00 am on January 24th, the party left their camp at Gum Hole. The skies were dark and rain was threatening. Hagarty wanted to reach the coast before noon. He noted that the country along the coast was 'very open; mainly beef wood sand hills and salt pans that were very boggy'.

Hagarty began to adopt a search strategy that would fully utilise his limited resources. It was an enveloping pattern of search, with two men working south to an apex of a mile or so, and the other two working north in a similar pattern, the two groups gradually converging. The routine was logical because of the absence of tracks and Hagarty knew that lost people or parties are notoriously unpredictable. The group held the pattern as long as the terrain allowed. Because of the recent rain, crossing the creeks became increasingly difficult. Wading across Browns Creek was easy enough, as was Rainbow Creek, but Moonlight Creek was another matter. Even at the narrowest juncture the party had to swim across — no easy matter for four men with fourteen horses and supplies.

Swimming across a creek was never a desirable option, but in this case it had its advantages. Most of the animals' underbellies were infested with March flies, and the water would bring relief. The mosquitoes were so rampant that Hagarty commented that they had become 'blood donors'. None of the men shaved. The facial hair protected them against flies, bugs and mosquitoes. A dip in the water was also a relief from the heat and humidity.

When Hagarty saw the swollen banks of Moonlight Creek, he knew that they couldn't simply swim across. If they did get across they might lose or injure an animal, or worse. There was no question that many of the supplies, from the flour to the ammunition, would be affected by water immersion. Hagarty devised a plan. He stripped the animals of the saddles and supplies. A makeshift raft was constructed; Hagarty called it a 'saddle boat'. The saddles were attached to a tarpaulin and the supplies were fastened to it. The horses crossed first, Hagarty in the lead and Marsh on the tail. When both men and animals could no longer ground their feet, the formation had to swim. If there was to be a disaster then it would occur now. Fortunately it was not long before the group touched the bottom and were soon across. Norman and Archie were already in the water. They had stripped naked. Their clothes were thrown onto the saddle boat. Both men grasped a corner of the raft and dog-paddled across to the other side.

Marsh watched the raft reach the bank and the two men walk from the water. The two trackers might have removed all of their clothes but their hats remained firmly attached to their heads. Marsh could not control his laughter.

The party soon reformed and were once again on their way. It had taken three hours to negotiate the fifty metres of Moonlight Creek, and by the time they made camp at a place called Round Hole, it was 8.00 pm. Marsh reckoned that they had made twenty-eight miles since leaving the morning camp.

The party made an early start the next morning. By 6.30 am, the four men and the fourteen horses were fed, packed and ready to leave Round Hole. The country searched was similar to that on previous days — vast, thick, uninhabited and seemingly endless.

It was not just the country that was becoming an adversary; ill fortune became an unwanted antagonist. Three hours after leaving camp, the men were startled when Buckle, a pack horse, reared up and broke formation. Animals and men went in all directions; supplies became airborne and Buckle galloped into thick scrub.

'Quick! Get the horses, hold them, hold them, watch the rations,' bellowed Hagarty. The two Aboriginals were soon in hot pursuit of the animals. It was a shambles and it was an hour before the horses were retrieved and re-formed. Hagarty and Marsh tracked Buckle into the bush and soon found the animal down and distressed.

'I think Buckle has been bitten by a snake — a king brown. I saw one crawl into the bush,' said Marsh. Hagarty knew what had to be done.

He reached for his Martini-Enfield and shot the animal dead. 'I hate losing a good horse,' he told Marsh. 'It's like losing a good friend. This animal never put a foot wrong. You can't help getting attached to a good horse.'

Startled by the gunshot, Norman had raced to the scene. Archie was taking care of the horses. The three men gathered up the scattered supplies, saving what they could. It was a bad morning.

In the early afternoon the trek continued on its way. At 2.00 pm they crossed Doomadgee Creek in conventional fashion. Two hours later the Dulwidgee Creek offered a similar scenario to Moonlight Creek and it was time to tie the horses together and construct the saddle boat. This time the roles were reversed. Norman and Archie took the horses across and Hagarty and Marsh, keeping their hats and clothes on, paddled the raft to the other side. The party eventually made camp at 7 o'clock near a place called Gingulla Hole. It had been a long day. Marsh calculated that they had travelled thirty miles, and had found no further trace of the Americans.

'Bob, we must be well and truly into the Territory by now. It would be eighty miles from the plane. Do you really think that they are still alive?' asked Marsh.

'Boss, even blackfellas don't come here,' said Archie. 'The white-fellas from the plane, they got no water, no tucker.'

'If they are alive, we're the only hope that they have,' said Hagarty. 'Maybe they're dead or dying. The crocs might even have got them. We'll give it a few more days and then go to Wollogorang Station and see Duncan McLean. He'll give us fresh horses and some food. We can rest there a while. Perhaps he might have heard something about the Yanks.'

The weather was fine on January 26th and the men had breakfast early. They badly needed fresh supplies. Everything was in short supply, including, as Hagarty feared, the men's resolve to continue the search. By 7.00 am they had packed and were heading for Cliffdale Creek, one of the largest in the area. Once there, they knew that another swim was in store. It was crocodile country and Hagarty knew that a confrontation was possible. It was to be hoped that it wouldn't be while they were in the water.

The bush was once again unforgiving. Hagarty wrote in his diary:

The country in places defies imagination and description, harbouring every type of pest that flew or crawled. We spelled the horses frequently, but the heavy going, frequent swims were taking their toll. The incessant torture of March flies and mosquitoes didn't help much either. The horses and men are always accompanied by a faint misty haze of mosquitoes.

It was not just the flies and mosquitoes that constantly plagued the men and animals. At noon that day Hagarty heard the buzz of wasps. Almost immediately, another pack horse jumped out of line and galloped into the dense undergrowth.

'Jitter's been stung,' Hagarty called out. 'Stay here, I'll get him.' Before he could pursue the horse, the men heard a shriek coming from the bush. It was the unmistakable sound of an animal in agony. Jitter had run into a broken tree limb and was impaled through the soft underbelly in front of the saddle sheath. Hagarty once again reached for his Martini-Enfield. Another horse down and at least two more lame. There's a limit to all of this, he thought.

To add to their woes the rain came pelting down, the first fall in the area in weeks. At least they would get some fresh water, but Hagarty knew that any tracks that existed would soon be obliterated. He wondered what else could go wrong.

'Hey Boss, over here. I've found something.' Archie had left his mount and had picked up something. He quickly brought the object to the others. Hagarty grabbed the item and looked at it from all angles. It was a pouch or vest of some kind, but it had been crudely modified.

'What is it, Bob?' asked Marsh.

'I dunno, but it's definitely from the plane,' said Hagarty. The item was not only hacked about; it had a water stain around the centre.

'Wait a minute. I know what it is. It's a life vest or a life preserver. They carry it in case they go into the water. This one's been chopped up. Chopped up to carry water. The Yanks have dropped it. They've been here. Look for some tracks. There's got to be some other sign. Quick, before the rain sets in.'

Within the hour the men had picked up the unmistakable signs of footprints made by leather-soled shoes. They had once again found the tracks of the American airmen. 'These Americans must be game bastards,' said Hagarty. 'It's tough enough to travel this country on horseback with rations, but the Yanks have nothing. They're on foot and it must be nearly a hundred miles to the plane.'

Marsh recorded the details for his subsequent report:

It was between Gingulla Hole and Cliffdale Creek that we first saw traces of the tracks made by the survivors. They were first seen about a mile to the east of Cliffdale Creek, travelling right along the beach. We followed their tracks right to the bank of the creek, but they were very hard to see owing to the rain. We followed the tracks for about half a mile, but it was impossible to follow them after they left the saltpans. We crossed Cliffdale Creek and proceeded westwards along the coast for about five miles, where we camped about 7 pm. Distance travelled about 30 miles.

The next day Hagarty decided to take Norman and ride towards the area near Guagudda Creek. He left the pack horses and the other animals with Marsh and Archie. They could rest up for the day. Before continuing the search for the men, he wanted to check the southerly salt pans near the beach to make sure that the Americans did not change direction and head east. Once he eliminated this possibility he could search the beaches and inland areas to the west with all of his resources. It was a long day — twenty miles over salt pans, beach and shrub — but nothing was found. The two men returned to the camp at 8.30 pm.

Hagarty knew that he would need to obtain fresh supplies and give the party an extended rest. The men were weary and lacerated and their clothes were torn and shredded. The horses were no better. Some were lame and all were infested with insects and vermin. They had been in the bush for fifteen days and the supplies were all but gone. Since leaving Round Hole they had been augmenting their stock with bush food. Hagarty believed that Wollogorang Station was about a day's ride to the south-east — about twenty-five miles. First, he would rest up for a day. Marsh and Archie could a take a look to the north and the party would leave for Wollogorang when they returned.

It was 7.00 am on the morning of January 29th when Marsh and Archie left camp. Hagarty had instructed them to proceed west and search the coastal areas as far north as possible.

CHAPTER SIX

'*I don't want to spend another night in the open*'

GRADY GASTON had never been so frightened in his life. He knew that he would have to parachute from the aircraft, but he still hoped that the order would never come. 'Prepare to jump,' said Crosson. 'I'm taking her up to 9000. Put on your life vests. Make sure that it's inflated. We could be over water. I'm going to level out. When I give the order, everyone out.'

Nobody in the crew had used a parachute before. Some guys had served a career in the army without ever jumping, and here was the crew of *Little Eva* jumping on their first mission.

Gaston did not even know if he had put the chute on properly. He checked the harness and felt the buckles. Whatever happened he was not going to be the first one out of the ship. He waited at the bomb bay door and heard the wind whistling through the opening. Below was only darkness. Gaston saw Grimes and Dyer jump; he knew it would soon be his turn. A figure appeared behind him. It was Lieutenant Speltz. 'Out!' he said. 'Come on, jump. There's no time.' Gaston didn't know whether he jumped or was pushed — it made no difference. The first thing he noticed was the sensation of falling, both terrifying and compelling. His legs became animated, instinctively searching for firm ground. Gaston felt nothing beneath him, only the rush of cool air, and then it became quiet. The drone of the engines and the sounds of human confusion were replaced by a tranquil feeling of solitude. Everyone knew to count to three before pulling the ripcord, but Gaston could not even remember counting before the chute became engaged. The jolt temporarily took his breath away. It felt like someone had caught him and was pulling him back on to the plane. He grunted and gasped. Dangling like a puppet, he made fists around the upper harness. Maybe some of the others were close by, drifting and falling like him. 'Can anyone hear me?' he shouted. 'Hello, can anyone hear me? It's Grady.' There was no one. Then he heard a sound, away to the east, distant and distinctive, a scraping noise and then an explosion. It could only be the ship coming down.

Gaston didn't know what was below him — land or sea. He was no mariner. He hadn't even seen the ocean until he joined the army. Don't let it be the sea, he thought. He made sure that his vest was inflated. Everything was so dark. He wondered how long it would take to come down. Maybe I'm drifting away, he thought. Drifting with the wind — out to sea.

He felt the pain of impact of scraping twigs and broken branches. He instinctively brought his elbow up to cover his eyes. The jolt was worse as the chute became tangled in the branches. He felt a jabbing pain in his side. 'Oh God!' he shouted. 'God help me.' The seven-minute fall from 9000 feet had ended with Gaston still in the harness, hanging from a cluster of trees. He was going nowhere for the moment. He took some deep breaths and gave himself a minute or two to rest.

Removing himself from his harness and from the trees was no easy task. He was about to climb down the tree when he heard the unmistakable sound of exploding ammunition — undoubtedly 50 calibre. He stopped and spread some foliage and gazed in the direction of the sounds. He could see the flickering of a fire — it was the ship — a long way to the east, probably ten or twelve miles.

'Who's that!' yelled Gaston, startled and alarmed by a noise behind him. It sounded like somebody, or something, bustling through the bush. 'Is there somebody there?'

'It's Grimes — Lieutenant Grimes Who's that?'

'It's Gaston, sir — I'm in a tree. I'm coming down. Stay there. Don't move. I'm coming down.'

Gaston climbed down the tree and jumped to the ground. Grimes had landed nearby. He could hear the ammunition exploding, but could not see the fire. He began walking in the direction of the sounds, dragging his parachute. The men were pleased to see each other. The prospect of being alone in this place was too terrifying to contemplate.

'Is there anyone else around? Did anyone else make it?' asked Grimes.

'Just me,' said Gaston. 'I think I've hurt my side, but I'm okay. The ship came down to the east, maybe ten or fifteen miles from here. I could see the glare of the fire and hear the ammo going off. Wait a minute, did you hear that? … There's somebody else out there.'

Grimes had also heard the sounds. 'Over here … Who is it? We're over here.'

'Is that you, Dale? It's Speltz … I heard voices … Where are you? Is there anyone else with you?'

'Just me and Gaston … We're over here. Can you see us?'

It was the second and last reunion of the night. 'Has anyone seen the Skipper? Have you heard from anyone?' asked Speltz. 'Thank God we're okay. I thought that we might be over the sea. We would have been goners for sure. We've gotta' try and find the others — find the ship. Has anyone got a watch? … Does anyone know the time? How long do you figure till daybreak?'

Grimes told Speltz that it was around 3.00 am. It made no sense to wander around the bush in the dark. The men were stressed and exhausted. They knew that it would be better to get a couple of hours sleep and face things in the morning. Their ordeal over, the three men lay on the ground and wrapped themselves in the two surviving chutes. Too tired to care or protest, the men ignored the omnipresent mosquitoes, soon to become an unrelenting and merciless bush opponent.

The men rose at dawn to ponder the situation. There were more questions than answers. Where were they? Where were the others? What now?

'I think that we're near the north Queensland coast,' said Speltz. 'We couldn't get a bearing in the storm, so we could be anywhere. But my guess is that we're near the coast — somewhere near Cairns. Maybe we should find the sea and follow the coast, keep goin' north … Has anybody got a cigarette?'

'The Skipper and the others could be waiting with the ship,' said Gaston. 'I think that he told us to meet there as soon as we could. Maybe we should find the plane and meet up with the others.'

'In what direction?' said Grimes. 'It's miles away. There's no high ground here to get a bearing and we could spend days looking for it and still never find it. Maybe no one else made it. It could be just the three of us. I'm for getting outta' here. We should start for the coast — walk north-west. We'll probably walk into a homestead or something. I don't know about you guys, but I don't want to spend another night in the open. Let's have a look at what we've got. Does anyone have a kit?'

Survival training for the Army Air Corps personnel in the early days of the war was rare, if non-existent. Things were little better with the survival kits. Each man was supposed to be issued with survival rations stored in his parachute pack, with the inventory consisting of a hand gun with ten rounds, a jungle knife, a fishhook and line, water-proof matches, four bits of chocolate, some basic medical supplies and a small tube of morphine. However, most of the contents went missing before the kits made it to the front line. The morphine became so rare that any kit containing the drug became a collector's item. The men of the 90th Bomb Group were also issued with a survival pamphlet designed for New Guinea operations. On one side there were handy survival hints in English, with Pidgin English on the reverse. No one knew exactly where they were, but it sure as hell wasn't New Guinea.

Gaston was the only one who had a ration kit. Grimes had his chute but no rations. Speltz had neither. As they were pondering their provisions and their fate, they heard another voice. 'Hallo, Hallo. Is there any one there?'

The men saw a figure approach from the distance. It was John Dyer, the ship's navigator. There was joy and relief that another crew member was alive, but there would be no more calls from the bush. The four men were now alone.

The men formed a semicircle and the group's inventory was placed on the ground. There was little rejoicing: four bars of chocolate, one jungle knife and a few matches in a waterproof container. The only other implements that might assist them in their ordeal were the two .45 calibre hand guns that both Gaston and Dyer carried. It was a miserable collection of bits and pieces and a long way from the official survival gear that all should have carried. But no one was too concerned. The worst was over, they thought. They had lived to tell the tale and with luck they should be found by nightfall. It was 7.00 am when the men rose, gathered their items and began walking in a north-westerly direction.

It was hot. Gaston knew about heat. He had worked his daddy's fields in Alabama, picking cotton. There were few fields of any description where Speltz, Dyer and Grimes came from and none of them had ever picked cotton. Gaston thought that he was used to hot weather, but he had never felt anything like this. It was like standing next to an open fire. There was no breeze and the humidity was fierce. Gaston figured it to be around 105 degrees. It was time to jettison the thick clothing that they wore for altitude flying. Members of the AAF were issued with an olive-green flying suit that was made of medium-weight cloth. Whether you served in the ETO or the Pacific you received the same kit. Most of the 90th wore the cotton uniform, which had a short knot collar and knitted cuffs. This was all the covering anyone needed in warm temperatures. The fleece-lined boots and leather jackets were inappropriate for trekking in hot, open country. The four men took off their jackets, carried them for a spell and then let them drop on the saltpans west of Moonlight Creek.

The day wore on. The men looked into the distance for any sign of habitation and to the skies for any searching aircraft. No one knew whether the base had received the distress calls. Even if they had, there was no certainty that they would know where to search. The land was a constant paradox. The country was predominately flat and featureless, with trees that seldom grew more than a few feet in height. It was difficult to get a visual bearing, and in most directions you could see no further than fifty yards.

There was the occasional clearing with plenty of vegetation and then there was undergrowth so thick that you often had to squat on your knees to get through.

To complete the paradox, there were open, parched saltpans, where you could see for miles in either direction. If they were to be seen from the air, it would need to be in open country. Dyer had a small compass, which at the very least guaranteed that they would not walk around in circles. Because of the intense heat, the men had to rest often. The flies were bad, but the mosquitoes were worse. No one wanted to think about spending another night out there, but what everyone did think about was thirst. The men were parched. By late on the first day there was still no sign of water. Twilight made it cooler, but the dark made it menacing. For the first time in their lives the men had endured a full day without food or water.

Nightfall came and there was no rescue. None of the men had expected to spend another night in this place. Sleep was almost impossible. The mosquitoes were rampant. The men burrowed into the ground, shirt collars stretched to cover their faces. The humming cacophony was broken only when a frustrated airman slapped his skin in a forlorn attempt to repel the pests. The ground was hard, the bodies stiff and sore. Thirst, hunger and fear were omnipresent.

The morning broke and it was clear that it would be another hot day. The trek towards the coast continued. Dyer believed that it was not far away. Nobody talked much: the throats were too dry, the limbs too sore. The boots that Speltz wore had never been a good fit and what had previously been uncomfortable was now painful. The men would have traded their souls for a glass of cold water.

It was 10.00 am on the second day when they smelled the unmistakable scent of the ocean and heard sound of breakers. At last they had reached the coast. The four men ran through the undergrowth. What a sight to behold the beach and the sea. It was as if their ordeal was over.

The men gathered in a group. 'This has got to be the north Queensland coast. We've made the coast,' said Dyer. 'The question now is which way do we go. Cairns could be north or south. There's no bearing — nothing that looks familiar.'

'We've got to get help soon,' said Speltz. 'We need water. My feet are killing me. I can hardly walk.'

'North, I think we should go north,' said Grimes. 'Townsville is a lot further away and Townsville is definitely south. Do we all agree?'

'What difference does it make?' said Gaston. 'North or south, it's only a matter of time before we get picked up.' He was doing it hard. It was not just the heat, the walking, the thirst and the hunger; it was being stuck out here with three lieutenants. He had never had much to do with officers and now he felt uncomfortable. He had little in common with these men. They were all from the big cities and were educated and worldly. He was just a farm boy from Alabama.

'Okay, we'll rest up a bit and then go north,' said Dyer. 'We'd better stick as close to the coast as possible. We'll be easier to see that way — when our guys come looking.'

It must have been past noon before the men started north. It was tough walking on the sand, even tougher for Speltz who hobbled behind. He had taken off his boots and draped them around his neck. His feet felt the heat, but he thought it would be okay as long as they stayed on the beach.

'Water. I've found water,' yelled a triumphant Grimes. 'It's only a pond, but it's not salt water. I think that it's okay to drink.'

Grimes was pleased with himself. He had left the group to find water and he had succeeded. The water was stagnant, but it was drinkable, and that was all that mattered. The men converged on the water, virtually falling into the pool — all except Speltz who was more cautious.

'Watch out for the gators,' he said. 'I hear that there's gators around these parts.'

It didn't matter. Thirst prevailed and the gators were forgotten. The men drank quickly and almost threw-up. The water was anything but pure, but it didn't seem to be polluted. The need for water had been resolved. It was now hunger that gripped the men. None of them had eaten for forty-eight hours.

The men rested by the pool for the night. The mosquitoes, frequent pests at any time, infested the area. One way of escaping them was to cake the face and neck with mud; it was uncomfortable, but preferable to the mosquitoes. Flies too, were a constant menace, usually during the day. The fear of creepy, crawling predators like the reptiles seen at Iron Range never abated. Speltz never stopped worrying about crocodiles, the ultimate nemesis for a Minnesota freshman lost in the Australian outback.

Morning came and the men knew that water would be scarce. They had to find some way of taking water with them. No one had a canteen or any suitable container. It was Gaston who used the jungle knife to fashion a crude container from the top part of his life jacket.

The trek began again. It was as before, Grimes and Dyer in the lead. Gaston and Speltz, carrying the life jacket with its precious cargo bouncing and spilling out on to the ground, walked in the rear. The pace was slower because of Speltz's feet. He prayed that help would come soon. Only his hunger took his mind off the pain.

The direction was north to north-west. It was fortunate that they had the coast as a bearing, for Dyer had inadvertently dropped the compass in salt water and it was all but useless.

The men were surprised by the extremes that they would go to to gain relief from the effects of thirst and hunger. Ever since leaving for the coast they had sucked on moist leaves and chewed on green tree bark. It had been Gaston's idea, and it was unpleasant, unsavoury and generally unsuccessful. Although the thirst had been temporarily quenched, the hunger pains remained. No one had ever experienced such hunger. There were berries and some kind of wild fruit, but there was always trepidation when eating anything unknown. Most of the time it was spat out, followed by a selection of expletives.

Two days after reaching the coast, the search for food had taken the men inland. Dyer saw it first. A young bullock had strayed into the area. 'We can get close to it and kill it,' said Dyer.

'Be careful,' said Speltz. 'Maybe it's a long horn. Don't get too close. It's probably wild.'

'We'll have to shoot it,' said Gaston. 'Who's going to do it? Is any-body any good with a hand gun?'

Grimes drew his revolver. 'I'll do it. We'll have to come at it from all sides — make sure it doesn't get away.'

The men were startled by the sound of the gunshot. Grimes had
missed with the first shot. The trigger mechanism was stiff and he had
jerked the weapon. The bullock began to run. The men ran towards it
from three sides, waving their arms and yelling. Once again Grimes
raised the weapon. Gaston and Speltz placed their hands over their
ears. The revolver discharged and the animal shrieked and fell.
Grimes ran to the animal and killed it with another shot to the head.

Speltz was as desperate as he was decisive. He began to dissect the
animal. The knife was blunt and the work hard. It took an hour before
they were through. As they walked away carrying as many portions as
possible, they noticed that the carcass was already becoming food for
the crows. Other predators were there to savour the banquet and the
Americans were no different. They had become primal predators on
the food chain.

On the beach they collected wood for the fire and tried to light it.
The matches were standard issue and included in a small metal container in the survival kits. 'They're too damp,' said Dyer. 'The matches
are damp, damn it!'

No one wasted any more time. The flesh was eaten raw.

It was tough to chew and not easy to swallow, but it raised the men's
spirits. They didn't want to carry the flesh around any more, and
believing that they would soon be picked up, decided to leave it for
the bush animals.

As always, water again became a priority — not just for drinking
but also for washing. The men reeked of blood, particularly Speltz,
who was covered in blood and tissue. The scent drew the flies even
more than usually. There was plenty of water. Not just the sea, but a
seemingly endless number of creeks and rivers. Some could be waded
across. Others could only be crossed by swimming. It was the same
routine. The men waited and looked along the banks, looking for the
crocodiles that could pounce at any time. Then one of the men would
wade into the water and start swimming. The others followed,

looking straight ahead; nobody looked back or looked around. As soon as their feet touched bottom, they frantically climbed out of the water. Worse than the creek was the mud, which was often knee-deep. On many occasions they had to crawl thorough dense bush, which left them bruised and lacerated. The sun, too, was merciless; by the fourth day they were burnt and baked. They had fared better when searching for food. They now knew which fruit and berries could be eaten and Dyer had shot a couple of birds. They had used up most of the ammunition, but this didn't concern them — they were living for the moment.

Soon, all they had was the clothes on their backs. They carried no surplus gear. There was no need for jackets or life preservers, so the men had discarded them, along with the revolvers, which were heavy and had been rendered useless by water immersion.

On December 12th, ten days after the crash, Dyer saw a large fish lying on the beach. It looked like a swordfish and had probably been washed ashore during the night. It was still alive and moving. Gaston jumped onto the 'long bill' and Dyer plunged a knife into the head. Nobody tried to light a fire. The boy scout 'two sticks' method never worked. Their hands were too sore and no one had the patience for it. Raw fish was even worse than raw steer; it was tougher and it had more bones. The attempts at fishing at night were mostly futile. On the rare occasion when they landed a fish, there were shouts of jubilation. However, by December 13th all the hooks had gone, carried away from the tired hands and fingers into the deep. Someone had a safety pin that they structured into a hook, but it too vanished into the depths.

Speltz's condition was causing concern. It was clear that he could not venture much further. His feet were bloodied, swollen and infected. He lagged behind the others, limping and staring into Gaston's back, which was usually covered with flies, those big ferocious ones that gave the men no peace. The men were starting to feel that maybe they wouldn't get out of this after all, although no one gave voice to those feelings. Maybe they were going to die, in this God forsaken place and no one was ever going to find them.

It was hot and dry on the morning of December 18th, as the trek continued, with the men struggling in the bush, parallel to the shore. The beach had become too hot for the shoeless Speltz to walk on.

Gaston heard it first. He stopped and looked to the skies. He saw nothing, but he could hear something faintly in the distance. The others had heard it too. They searched the skies. It was difficult to see through the treetops, but there was an unmistakable sound of engines coming from the east.

'They're B-24s,' said Dyer. 'I can hear B-24s.'

Meanwhile, back at the range the 90th Bomb Group was still prosecuting the war. The mission of December 1st had become one of several that the group flew in the first weeks of December. Crosson and his crew were gone but not forgotten. Most feared that they had shared the same fate as Art Meehan's ship, *Punjab*, on November 17th. It was almost routine; if a ship took off for a mission and did not come back, it was listed missing in action. After two weeks, and still no news of Crosson's crew, the orderlies began gathering the men's belongings and the crew's names were forwarded to Base Section Three (Brisbane) and then to the War Department. Soon, relatives were notified that their boys were missing in action in the South West Pacific. A few weeks later the families received another telegram, confirming what was patently obvious: 'missing presumed dead'.

The 90th were continuing to learn the hard way. On December 7th, a year after the Pearl Harbor attack, the group was going to give the Japs 'hell'. Six Japanese destroyers were sighted running along the coast of New Britain.

'This raid will go down in history,' Rogers told his officers at the early morning briefing. 'This is our chance to hit the Japs for what they did to the navy at Pearl Harbor.'

The 320th Squadron was given the honour and the chance for glory. Once again there was only ignominy. Darkness fell before the ships could be spotted. Gasmata was the alternate target, but the cloudy and dark conditions made it impossible to pinpoint its position, and 36 000 lbs of high explosives fell into the water. Charles Whitlock wrote in his dairy: 'The Japs doubtless celebrated Pearl Harbor with a good fish fry.'

On that same day, the 321st did little better with a raid on Rabaul. The weather was once again the enemy. A lack of fuel and high-altitude icing cut short the mission. Rabaul had to be below, it wasn't and this time 30 000 lbs of high explosives fell into the jungle.

Things could only get better, and they did. On December 13th, Lieutenant Robert McWilliams and his crew spotted a Japanese convoy and radioed the position to Port Moresby. Although badly shot up, the crew maintained surveillance and shot down a 'Betty' bomber and possibly two Japanese fighters, winning the Silver Star for gallantry.

The weather was often foul and dangerous, but on a December 16th reconnaissance mission, Walter Higgins, in *Cow Town's Revenge*, experienced different conditions:

It was beautiful for a change. Near Manus Island we could see a tropical setting and sail boats in the harbor. It made us forget that there was a war going on and that the islands were occupied by the Japanese. The scene was rhapsodic. The day memorable. It was the only mission from Iron Range that we enjoyed.

When Higgins arrived back at the base he was told the incredible news that Norm Crosson had been found in the Australian bush, near a place called Burketown, and that he and a gunner called Wilson had wandered around for twelve days before being found by a farmer. The 90th were to commence searches in the area immediately for the rest of the crew. Walter Higgins, Jim McMurria and the others of the

321st knew that finding the men would be like finding a needle in a haystack. In fact, it was worse than that — first, they had to find the haystack. The Gulf area, north-west of Burketown, had been searched for days and nothing had been found. McMurria went much further. On December 16th he swore that he was as far south as Ayers Rock.

Like everything else in the army, there were search procedures. On normal searches over water, if looking for downed planes or rafts, the plane would fly at around a thousand feet. When flying a recon mission, the altitude would be around four or five thousand feet. Most pilots, if they were at a low or moderate altitude, generally flew near the base of the clouds. High-altitude horizontal flying allows searches to observe for several miles, but it becomes difficult to see small objects, particularly in rough country. For this search the 90th's pilots often flew at altitudes of 500 feet, which made it easier to see details on the ground, but the lower the flight the faster you had to look. It could only be effective if everyone was on the ball.

Higgins was getting towards the end of his search area. The longer they conducted search patterns, the more difficult it became; what with inattentive periods, sore eyes and the endless bush terrain. 'Hey Pappy, do you really think they're still alive?' asked his navigator.

'Just keep looking,' said Higgins. 'Just keep looking.'

Dyer, Speltz, Grimes and Gaston saw the formation coming from the east. They raced for a clearing and saw the B-24s. The aircraft were no higher than 1000 feet. There was frantic yelling and the waving of arms. Speltz hadn't moved so fast in days. The yelling did nothing to attract the attention of the aircraft, but the excitement was intense. The men jumped and stomped, and Gaston took off his shirt and waved it over his head.

'I saw guys looking out of the waist gunner's hatch,' said Gaston. 'They were looking this way. They had to have seen us. Do you think they saw us?'

'They'll come back to get a fix,' said Grimes. 'They'll be back. We'll wait here. They'll be back.'

The aircraft flew away from the trees and into the distance and the engine sounds grew faint. The men waited for the B24s to return. Time confirmed the worst. If they had been observed, there should have been some sign, and there was nothing. It was the men's worst moment since their ordeal began.

Gaston was the only one who kept track of the time and he knew exactly how long it had been since the crash. He was forever leaving signs. He carved details on trees, left marks in the dirt — anything that could be found. He had no idea where he was, but someone might know. It was worth a chance — anything was worth the chance.

'How long has it been?' asked Dyer. 'How long since the crash, how long since the ship went down? How long have we been stuck out here?'

'It's the 24th — the day before Christmas,' said Gaston.

'Christmas in this place, in the middle of nowhere,' said Dyer. 'I bet that they've even stopped looking. We're finished.'

'We've got to stick together,' said Grimes. 'We'll rest a spell, but we've got to keep going. We can't give up. Our luck's gotta' change.'

The trek continued, once again parallel to the shore, but the men's resolve and motivation were fading. After three weeks in the wilderness, they were showing the effects of malnutrition: cheilosis of the corners of the mouth, red swollen papillae on the tongue, spongy, bleeding gums, poor muscle tone, hyperesthesia of the skin, dermatitis on most parts of the body, purple spots on the skin due to minute hemorrhages. It was only the beginning. Soon the men suffered from anemia, bloodshot eyes and scrotum infection, together with ever diminishing energy and strength. Inadequate nutrition was forcing the body to break down its own tissues in order to obtain the essentials needed for metabolism. The emotional trauma was no better. The prospect of spending Christmas in the wild, without shelter, food or hope, was the latest in a never-ending catalogue of emotional adversity.

At first they thought that they were seeing things. For the first time in twenty-one days the men were seeing something man-made. It looked like a small house, like a hut, and it was close to the shore. The men rushed towards it as quickly as their weary limbs would allow.

Dyer forced the door open. Once again their sprits plummeted. It was only a paperbark shack, no more than ten feet square. It was obvious that no one had been there for some time. There was no floor, but the roof gave them shelter from the sun.

'I'm for staying here for a while,' Grimes said. 'At least we have a roof over our heads for Christmas. Maybe someone will show up eventually.'

'I second that,' said Speltz. 'I've gotta' rest my feet. I ain't going no further till my feet get better.'

The area was no worse and was, in fact, a great deal better than most of the spots they had used since the crash. There was a small melon vine growing at the rear of the hut. The melons were tiny, but full of juice. As always there were plenty of berries around and the beach yielded a supply of dead fish, or small moving sand crabs.

On Christmas Day the men spent their time sitting in the hut, and at night they sang carols. The occasion produced a sombre bonding. Dyer spoke about his hometown of Lawrence in Massachusetts and of visits to Hampton Beach. Grimes was from Massachusetts, but had been born and raised in Boston. He claimed to have ancestors going back as far as the *Mayflower* and Plymouth Rock. Speltz said that if he had one wish it would be to tell his family that he was still alive and was thinking about them. He remembered the letter he'd posted to his mother on November 3rd. In it he had enclosed a cheque for $45, for his nieces and nephews. 'Get them something for Christmas, either a big thing, or two small things,' he'd written. Billy, Betty and Laurette were to get $10 each, and the younger children, Stan, Ang and Mary, $5 each. Gaston spoke about Frisco City and life on the farm, of Alabama when the crepe myrtle was in bloom, of walking down a shady street to the drugstore. He wondered what his mother had been told about his fate.

The singing didn't last long; only Speltz knew more than a couple of carols, so the others just hummed along. They prayed as a group, often saying the same prayer continuously. None of them had ever been so committed to their devotions as they were this day.

There were periods of intense solitude, with each man alone with his thoughts. The spirit of the occasion rallied the men as they tried to forget about their predicament; they even found time for hope. For a brief period that Christmas Day in 1942, they even forgot that they were dying.

CHAPTER SEVEN

'Help me. I'm in trouble'

THE occasion of Christmas not only brought a brief respite for the men, it also brought rain. The downpour was unrelenting. The shack leaked and the ground became damp, adding to the men's misery. The men discussed their plight. The ordeal had dispelled the bureaucracy of rank and the formality of authority; it had become a democratic foursome. They called each other by their first names. It seemed pointless to do otherwise. There was no precedent for their predicament, and the need for discipline was less important than the need for bonding.

Grimes seemed to be the fittest and the most committed. He wanted to push on. But Speltz's feet were still lacerated, infected and swollen, and for the time being he had to stay where he was.

The rain persisted until December 27th. On that day Grimes, Dyer and Gaston decided to continue north-west, leaving Speltz in the hut to rest his feet. The three men hoped to return with help or, at the very least, with some food. The choice to stay or to continue the trek had become academic; if they stayed, they would surely starve to death.

It was mid-morning and overcast when Grimes, Gaston and Dyer walked away from the hut and into the wild. Speltz had seen them off. The routine was as before — Grimes in front, Dyer behind him and

Gaston in the rear. They could make better time with no Speltz to hold them back.

No one was surprised when they encountered another river. They had crossed many since the trek began. Most were just creeks that they could simply wade across, but this one was different. The minute he saw it, Gaston was filled with trepidation about the prospects of getting across. It was easily the biggest river that they had seen since December 2nd. Although it was narrow in places, it was bloated from the recent rain, particularly where it flowed into the sea. The men waited at the river's edge, pondering their next move. There seemed little choice; they either had to cross it or go back. Once or twice in the past, when the water had been too deep, the men had taken off their shirts and wrapped them around some branches to make a makeshift raft. They had been pleased with their ingenuity, but no one relished using the technique to cross a true river with currents and crocodiles. Also, their clothes were now nothing more than rags and no one had the energy to construct such an apparatus.

Gaston suggested that they wait until the water dropped, but Dyer pointed out that it could take days. 'If we take our time and cross in the right place, we should be okay,' said Dyer. 'It looks okay right about here.'

Dyer took the lead and was the first one across. The water reached his chest, but he kept his footing. 'Come on, hurry up,' he yelled from the other side. 'Make sure that you stay on your feet.'

Gaston followed in the steps of Dyer. He had never been much of a swimmer. Wading across was okay, but he dreaded losing his footing. He could feel a current below his waist and it frightened him. He was relieved to reach the other side and wasted no time in climbing up the bank and shaking his clothing beside Dyer. Grimes was already in the water. He had become frustrated at the slow progress of Gaston and waded a few yards downstream to cross parallel to the others. There was also the temptation of a melon vine, looking healthy and hanging on the bank near the others. The others had seen it too, but the river was too wide and Dyer had sensed menace. The fruit could be picked later — better to get on the other side first.

'Something's wrong,' said Gaston. 'Dale's in trouble. He's going the wrong way.'

Grimes was still stroking, but making no forward progress. Still thirty yards from the shore, he seemed to be moving sideways. Something was indeed very wrong.

'The current's got him,' said Dyer. 'Dale! This way. Come this way. We're over here.'

Grimes muttered something, stopped momentarily and then waved his arms above his head.

'Help me,' he cried. 'I'm in trouble.' He disappeared below the water and then surfaced again. He was definitely out of his depth. Soon he was almost out of sight — thirty, forty and then fifty yards away from the others. He was no longer swimming in their direction. He had lost all his strength and began drifting helplessly with the tide. Gaston began running along the river bank parallel with Grimes. When he was almost level with him, he jumped into the water, but was afraid to venture further than waist-deep. The current was strong; it was swirling around his waist and between his legs. If he lost his footing, he would lose his life.

Dyer began looking for something that could be used as a life preserver — something to throw to Grimes — but there was nothing. By the time he joined Gaston, Grimes was almost out of sight. 'Hang on, we'll get you. Hang on, Dale.' The figure, by now in midstream, could only raise his left arm. Then he was gone. The men heard and saw nothing. It had only taken a few seconds.

'Maybe he can make it across upstream,' said Gaston. 'He can still make it.' There was no more upstream, only the sea, and the men knew it was hopeless. Dale Grimes was gone, drowned in this God-forsaken place.

The two men were motionless; neither said anything. There was shock, anger and disbelief. Gaston could hardly control his weeping — not only for Grimes, but for the others and for himself. He now felt sure that they were all going to die.

Gaston wanted to go back to the shack, but Dyer wanted to push on. At least they could make sure that Dale's death was not in vain. He had always been the one who wanted to push on. He was the shining light, the optimist. 'Gotta keep moving,' he would say.

Dyer knew that if Dale had survived, he would have pushed on regardless.

'We'll move north,' Dyer told Gaston. 'Maybe there's a town or something. How can anybody walk as far as we have without running into something? What kinda' country is this?'

It had been twenty-five days since the crash, and at this stage of the ordeal there was more resting than walking. Dyer and Gaston could scarcely cover a mile in an hour. Their strength was being sapped and they were growing weaker by the day.

The ultimate result of malnutrition is auto cannibalism — the body literally begins to devour itself. A body experiencing starvation will begin to consume its body fat in order to survive. When the fat is gone, the body will digest the muscles, resulting in drastic weight loss and the further destruction of the immune system. As the muscles are sacrificed for survival, any form of physical activity, even walking, becomes a major test of endurance. The body will continue its ravenous course of self-destruction. The organs are next: stomach, kidneys and liver begin to malfunction. Eyesight, coordination and then mental capacity become affected. The body temperature and blood pressure start to drop. Glands become inactive, before ceasing to work entirely. Physical collapse and cardiac arrhythmia are next. Without food, the body will continue to devour itself until death ends the suffering.

As Dyer and Gaston struggled northwards, their condition grew worse. Even with the bush fruit and the odd snail, lizard, crab or beached fish, they would seldom exceed 500 calories a day. After a while even eating became a major challenge, but worse was to come. After walking for another day the shoreline ended completely. Soon Dyer and Gaston became waist-deep in mud thorns and marshes. There was nothing ahead, only more suffering and death.

The men sat for a while and then decided to return to the shack, to rejoin Speltz. There was no other choice. They had to rest more and more. They decided to keep to the shoreline where possible, as it would be easier for them to be seen. Rescue was now considered remote. It had been nearly four weeks, and if they were going to be found, then it should have happened by now. They didn't even know where they were, but it didn't matter; they were going back to join Speltz in the shack and wait to die. At least their suffering would end. Grimes would suffer no more, and maybe Speltz had died too. It had been three days since they had left. Maybe he had found help and was waiting for them to return. But Gaston no longer embraced optimism. 'Right now,' he told Dyer, 'if it means getting out of here, I would even settle for the Japs.'

The men had walked twenty miles before deciding to turn back. It was the ultimate frustration, walking to the point of exhaustion and then going back to where it all started. Iron Range was a paradise compared with this place. The return trip to the old shack was going to take twice as long, but neither man cared — there was no need to rush. From now on there was no need to do anything. The men were losing control over their own destiny.

The heat from the sand made walking uncomfortable, but it was still better to stay on the beach, just in case someone spotted them from the sea or from the air. Not that they held out much hope of rescue. They hadn't had any luck since the mission a month ago, just thirty days of pain and suffering. It seemed that it could only get worse. They cautiously waded across the big river again, but this time they were further inland. It was noon when they reached the coast. Neither man spoke as they headed south — back to where they had started.

Both men saw the form at once. It was about a hundred yards away, lying on the beach, just ahead of the breakers. Gaston thought that it might have been some kind of fish, a big one — maybe a shark — washed ashore during the night. But this was no fish; it was the body of Dale Grimes, lying face down in the sand.

'Leave him alone,' said Dyer, as Gaston approached the body. 'Remember what we agreed on when we were all together. Leave him alone.'

When the men had been celebrating Christmas at the shack, it was Grimes who had suggested that if any of them died, they should be left where they fell. It was a tough call, but it was felt that a body might lead the searchers to the others. All had agreed and Grimes, the instigator of the idea, had become the first marker.

Dyer and Gaston were relieved that they did not have to bury Dale, as they no longer had the strength or the will. They left Grimes where he lay. Neither looked back.

It was late in the afternoon when they reached the shack, and the faint hope that rescuers might be waiting was soon dashed. Speltz was also hoping that the men would return with help. That wasn't the case; in fact there were only two of them. Where was Grimes? he wanted to know.

Dyer told him the grim news and Speltz could only shake his head in disbelief. The first of them had died and he knew that there would be more. Gaston tried to enliven the gloom. 'Arthur, I brought you some cockles I found near the beach. They'll make you feel better.'

Speltz quickly disposed of the feast, having not eaten for two days. 'They tasted as good as steak,' he told Gaston.

The year 1942 was almost gone, only two days left. No one was thinking about walking out of this place any more. It was now all about survival; food and water, that's all that mattered.

'What's that you're doing? What are you doing with the knife?' asked Dyer.

'I'm trying to leave a message on this coconut shell,' said Gaston. 'The next time that we go to get water I'll leave it on the ground. Someone could find it and know that we're still around.'

'Ain't no one going to find us here,' said Dyer. 'They've all finished looking. They've given us up for dead. We're finished.'

'You keep doing what you think is best, Grady,' said Speltz. 'I'm with you. Just keep leaving clues. What have we got to lose?'

Ever since the crash Gaston had been leaving signs of the wandering quartet, from broken twigs to articles of clothing. He was not full of hope, but he didn't share the pessimism of Dyer. Carving details of their plight on the face of an eight-inch by three-inch shell was no small task. The knife was blunt and his hands were tender. It took a whole day before it was finished.

'Take a look,' he said to Dyer and Speltz. 'If you guys can understand what's on here then anyone can. Take a look — see if you can make it out.'

US Army B24. Lt Grimes (N) Lt Dyer (B) Lt Speltz (CP) Sgt Gaston (R) Bailed out Dec 4, 1942 Reached here Dec 24, 1942. Grimes deceased Dec 27, 1942 Speltz, Grimes, Gaston forced to turn back Dec 30.

'It's okay, but the date's wrong,' said Speltz. 'We bailed out early on the day after the mission. It was December 2nd.'

'What does it matter what day it was?' said Dyer. 'Who cares?'

The nearest water was about four miles away from the shack. It was an ordeal just to make it that far. It felt like forty miles. Speltz had recovered enough to join the two men on their regular treks for food and water. He didn't like being left alone in the shack. He wanted to help, and; besides, his feet felt better. Water was not a major problem — the rain had filled the creeks and ponds — but food was becoming scarce. The men soon tired of the berries and bush fruit, and they wanted something more substantial. They had scavenged all they could from the area near the shack. Dyer believed that a better source of food lay to the north-west, but between the men and the possibility of food lay the big river — the one that had claimed the life of Dale. Gaston never wanted to see it again, let alone cross it, but Dyer persisted, suggesting that the water might have dropped since the first crossing. It hadn't rained a lot much since.

The men set off north on the first day of 1943. About two miles from the shack, Gaston walked a few yards into the bush and placed his shell next to a large tree. Dyer laughed out loud.

The water level of the river had receded, but it still reflected menace. No one had the energy to walk inland to find the narrows again, and Speltz was in no condition for an inland trek.

Gaston was frightened. He wasn't convinced that it was worth the risk to cross the river in search of a food supply that may not be there, but Dyer was persuasive and soon the three men started to wade into the river. The crossing was at the most narrow point, but it was still thirty to forty yards across.

'Why don't we go back and head east,' said Gaston. 'Maybe we can find some food there. Arthur may not be able to make it across.'

'No, I'm okay,' said Speltz. 'Let's give it a chance. We might even be able to find some help. We might run into somebody. It's worth the chance.'

Dyer waded in first, with Gaston a few feet behind. Dyer was soon waist-deep in the water, about fifteen yards from the shore. He stopped, and for a few moments remained motionless. Then suddenly he seemed to slip, as if he had tripped over something, and began bouncing up and down in the water. He had lost his footing. His torso rose and fell and his arms were splashing — he was in trouble.

Speltz thought that a crocodile had attacked him, but Gaston knew immediately that Dyer was caught in a fast-flowing current. It was the Grimes situation all over again. Instinctively, Gaston moved towards Dyer and extended his hand. Dyer grasped it firmly — too firmly and neither man could retain his footing. The current was fierce. Gaston went under, came up and then went under again. He could see downstream. He was being carried out to sea. Dyer still gripped his hand, locking the men together in a vice-like state of fear. Gaston was swallowing water and he couldn't find his feet. Dyer was dragging him downstream and he was sure he was going to drown. He was becoming too weak to struggle. The moments seemed like hours. Gaston could hear Dyer calling out for help, his voice full of terror. Still they held on to each other.

Speltz had seen the predicament and had waded back to the shore. He moved upstream as quickly as his fragile feet would allow. He kept ahead of the struggling, thrashing men, who were only a few yards from the shore. He entered the water just ahead of Gaston and Dyer and grabbed on to a protruding tree branch. He thought that with luck he might just reach them. He waded as deep as he dared, but did not let go of the branch. He dug his heels into the soft sand. His belt was in his hand, the buckle wrapped around his wrist. He could almost touch Dyer. There would be only one chance to do this. 'Grab the belt, John. Quick, reach out and grab the belt.'

Speltz felt tension on the belt. It nearly pulled him off his feet. His arms hurt; but he knew he must hang on. For a moment he thought that he was going to join the others in a journey down the river, but he held firm. Gaston's feet were moving as if he were riding a bicycle. He was about to give up when he felt the sand under his feet. He had found his footing. Dyer had as well and the two wasted no time getting out of the water. There was a rapid movement of limbs and bodies. Gaston collapsed on to the shore. He had never been so scared in all his life. It had been even worse than jumping from the ship. He'd been sure he was going to die.

Soon he was joined by the others. They had made it back to the original side of the river. 'That's it,' shouted Gaston. 'I'm never going to cross another river again as long as I live. No more swimming. I didn't join the army to drown in some lousy river. To hell with this. I'll take my chances back at the cabin.'

There was no response — only tacit agreement. After waiting a while the three men started to walk south, back to the shack. Nobody wanted to talk and no one wanted to go anywhere near where the body of Dale Grimes lay.

It is not known how the town of Borroloola got its name, only that it is an Aboriginal word. Some said that the word means 'tea-tree', others said that it means 'place of the paperbarks', but most said it meant nothing and most thought that living in Borroloola meant nothing.

Located 600 miles south-east of Darwin, the town is situated on the McArthur River, in the middle of nowhere, isolated and detached. Although the town belongs to the Barkley Tablelands area of the Northern Territory, its vegetation and climate are more relevant to the tropical Gulf savanna, which stretches around the Gulf of Carpentaria from North Queensland. The town was first established shortly after the intrepid explorer Ludwig Leichhardt passed through the area on his way to Queensland in 1845. Thirty years later, the famous 'overlander' Wentworth D'Arcy Uhr passed through the area with a large herd of cattle. The area soon became the apex of a familiar cattle route from Queensland to the Northern Territory. In 1885, the town was a supply base and port for drovers and selectors. A survey team led by a J. P. Hingston arrived in the town and left it with the name of Borroloola.

By 1890 the town had the obligatory pub, post office, butcher shop and general store. By the turn of the century the town had earned a reputation for total disrepute. Drovers moving cattle between the Kimberleys and western Queensland stopped in the town, and a trade in rum, smuggled from Thursday Island, was established. This illicit trade soon attracted undesirables to the town. Borroloola became a centre for felons and alcoholics. The town boasted some legendary names — Orphan Jack Martin, Pigweed Harry Herbert, Billy 'the Informer' Hynes, Big Eyed Billy, and Old Billy McLeod, who was said to be the best bushman and the 'whitest' man in the Territory. There was a cosmopolitan flavour as well. The American schooner, *Good Intent*, sailed up the river in 1931, under the command of a man called Black Jack Reid. The first mate answered to the name of 'Smoked Beef', whose presence was a constant source of interest to the townsfolk. He was black, but he did not look like an Aboriginal — he was a black American.

The small town was not without an element of culture. Cornelius Power, the resident officer of the Borroloola Police Station, established a town library. He was granted a small sum of money and began ordering books from Mudie's Select Library in London. By the 1920s the town had over 3000 volumes, the biggest collection in the Territory. It is said that Power was in Borroloola long enough to read every book twice.

Borroloola was a true frontier town, but times change and the droving routes changed and Borroloola became a ghost town. Since 1935, no one visited Borroloola who didn't have to.

Edward Heathcock was not in the town during the 'good old days', but he knew about the myths and stories. He had been the constable at the Borroloola Police Station since 1938. He had arrived soon after a cyclone had damaged the town, taking the roof clean off the Tattersalls Hotel.

Heathcock had been a police officer for fifteen years and at forty-nine he still enjoyed the rank of constable, but in Borroloola it meant something. He was the law in the town; in fact he was the only law for hundreds of miles. The nearest policemen were Ted Small at Daly Waters to the south-west and Harry Nuss at Burketown, 200 miles to the south-east.

Heathcock enjoyed the mounted patrols. He was a familiar figure at the nearby Roper River Mission, and during his visits he often stayed two or three days. It was not all business. During the lunch hours, he would sit under a big paperbark tree and reach for his mouth organ, which he played with great enthusiasm. He was no virtuoso, but he was no mug either. The sound of his playing would be like a magnet for the Aboriginal children, who quickly gathered around him as he played. They particularly enjoyed his rendition of 'Lead Kindly Light'.

Between recitals, he told them of his experiences in the Great War. Heathcock had been one of the first men ashore at Gallipoli, and during the campaign had been shot in the chest, almost fatally. Seldom a day went by that he did not feel the pain of his wounds, pain that grew worse as he got older. 'White boss Ted' was a great storyteller. As he regaled the children with stories of battles won and mates lost, tears would run down his cheeks. The children cried too.

Heathcock's terrier, Trixie, was a constant companion. The children loved to watch the constable mount his horse, whistle for the dog, and with one swoop of his hand catch the leaping animal and place it in front of his saddle. The pair would trot off into the distance, with the children following. Ted Heathcock was always welcome at Roper Mission.

Heathcock was content to see out the war in Borroloola. Not that you knew that there was a war on. The town was as isolated as any in the country. News about the war, or anything else, was intermittent. The post office had a facility to send telegrams, which was the medium for Heathcock to report urgent matters to Superintendent

Stretton at Police Headquarters in Alice Springs, 400 miles away. But there was little contact with Stretton, because very little happened. Any reports that he composed were sent by mail, which left once a week. An urgent communiqué could be sent by telegram, but he never had any reason to send one. Any trouble in this place usually had something to do with the blacks. The Yanyuwa, Mara, Karawa and Kurdanji people all lived in or near the town.

In 1943 there were only about fifty people living in Borroloola, not counting the blacks — no one in the territory, or in Australia for that matter, ever counted the blacks. Ted Heathcock was content in this place where nothing ever happened. Then on 5 February 1943, everything changed.

An Aboriginal called Tommy arrived in the town by canoe from the Robinson River. He rushed to the police station and began telling Heathcock about something he had seen the day before near Seven Emus Station. While walking along the beach between the Robinson and Wearyan rivers, he had found the remains of a body, partly buried in the sand. He believed that it was a white man, because the body was still clad in the remnants of a uniform.

Heathcock questioned Tommy at length, but there seemed to be little doubt about the validity of the story. He rushed to the post office to send a telegram to Stretton.

Heathcock knew that he now had to deal with something that was not only significant but also potentially important. Tommy's description suggested that the body was that of a serviceman. But why was it in an area so distant from anywhere and so desolate?

Heathcock decided to demonstrate some initiative. He sent word to Owen Cole, a lieutenant at the nearby military base. He did not ask for any assistance from the soldiers — it was a civil matter and under police jurisdiction — but he promised Cole that he would report any further events. Cole told Heathcock that he did not believe the body to be that of an Australian serviceman, unless it had been washed ashore from a ship or an aircraft. He did, however, suggest that it might be connected with an incident involving a crashed American bomber that he had heard about.

'Some of the crew were never found,' he said, 'but it's in the wrong area. There's no way they could have walked that far — it must be 100 miles from where they came down.'

Heathcock sent word to Stretton that he was going to make a patrol of the area, leaving as early as possible on the 7th. There wasn't time to organise a party. Good men were scarce, and the homesteads were too few and too distant. Even Trixie was to stay at home. Heathcock would need Tommy to show the way, and he asked a local black, Charlie Yambarna, to assist. Charlie was an excellent bushman.

He decided to take as many horses as possible. If it was one of the lost Americans, there was a possibility that he might find the rest. It was better to have the horses and not need them, than to need them and not have them.

Heathcock and the two Aboriginals gathered and saddled Sting, Bailif, Bradman, Bobby, Scent, Victim, Caress and Blossom. They were good mounts, healthy and strong, as were the three pack mules, Bella, Clara and Bushranger. It was a little after 9am before the group left Borroloola. Heathcock did not want to waste any more time. With luck, they could make it to Fletcher Creek before nightfall.

The group did make it to Fletcher Creek as the sun set. It was good progress. They did even better the next day, making Snake Lagoon by 5.00 pm, giving them plenty of time to make camp. Heathcock knew that they could make Horse Creek by nightfall on the third day, and from there it was only a few miles to where Tommy had found the body.

The nights were long and Heathcock missed the company of white men. Unlike Bob Hagarty, he was not an expert bushman, or someone who had empathy with blacks. He had nothing against them, but neither did he have anything in common with them. He spent the time questioning Tommy at length about the area and about the find.

It was not until the third night of the journey that Tommy confessed that he had moved the remains from the beach, placed them in a bag and pushed them into a large casuarina tree. Heathcock was aghast. The scene where the body was found could provide valuable clues as to the identity and the circumstances relating to the death. Perhaps it was foul play and he fell where he was killed. Now, no one would ever know.

'Why did you move the body?' he asked Tommy. 'Why did you move the whitefella's bones?'

'I didn't want anyone to steal them,' said Tommy. 'I wanted to hide them. Dingoes could take them. I went back and got a bag. I didn't tell anyone — no blackfellas. This was whiteman police business. I put the bones in a safe place — in a tree — I know where they are. I can find the tree.'

Heathcock knew that it was now academic. A potential crime scene had been disturbed and the evidence compromised, but perhaps Tommy was right. The remains could have been washed away or ravaged by animals.

As he promised, Tommy had no difficulty in finding the tree. Soon the three men were underneath the casuarina's foliage. Heathcock looked high up into the tree. Hanging from a protruding branch was a large bag firmly tied to the limb. Tommy was soon climbing the tree and in a matter of minutes the bag was at the feet of Heathcock. He initially thought that he should return with the bag unopened, but then decided that if anything was missing from the body it might be found in the area.

Heathcock carefully opened the bag onto a blanket that he had spread under the tree. It was a distressing moment. He knew that it was important to carefully catalogue the remains — he did not want to have any problems with Stretton — and to follow the appropriate procedures. With two very curious onlookers Heathcock began to examine the remains. He took his time. He had a number of pencils and an old school pad in which to document his finding. He needed to be thorough. He assiduously took notes as he knew that a report would be required.

The first thing that he noticed was that the remains were by no means complete. Most of the bones were missing and very little flesh remained. Heathcock assumed that the body had been consumed by scavengers. The bones that were there had been bleached white by the sun.

There was one upper arm, two lower leg bones, eight pieces of backbone, six ribs, one shoulder blade, a skull with lower jaw and a full set of teeth. He noted that the teeth were in excellent condition — only one or two fillings. Heathcock had long since lost his teeth and now wore dentures.

He carefully measured the bones and examined the clothing. The khaki shirt and trouser legs were practically rotten. On the collar of the shirt he noted a badge that resembled a pair of wings and a propeller. There was also an oblong badge about an inch long and half an inch wide that appeared to be a badge of rank. The shirt was a size seven with a name stamped on it. Heathcock could barely make it out — D.V. 'Ghime' or 'Simes' or perhaps it was 'Grimes'.

It was obvious that the body was that of an American officer and aviator. He could have been washed up from the sea, a victim from a crash out to sea. Could he have been from the Liberator bomber? wondered Heathcock, but that was in North Queensland, hundreds of miles away and months ago. Heathcock wished that he had the names of the missing flyers.

The clothing contained a web belt in good condition with a sliding metal buckle. The shirt was a long-sleeve type with double buttons on the wrists. The shoe was a size ten, brown in colour with a rubber heel. Heathcock carefully went through the pockets, which were full of holes and sand. Along with a small comb, he found four shillings and three pence. This was Australian currency, so the American had been based in Australia.

Heathcock knew that he had stumbled across something important and that he would need to report to Stretton as soon as possible. This could only be done back at the station, but the scene could still hold some clues and Heathcock wanted to search the area. Perhaps there were more bodies. He had travelled this far, and did not want to waste the opportunity. It was mid-afternoon. He had to make a choice: start for home or camp here. While he pondered the situation, Tommy suggested another option: he knew about an old hut in the area, a little to the south, that they could stay in while they conducted a search.

'Boss Jack built it for the boys to stay in while chasing cattle,' said Tommy. 'Boss Jack' was Jack Keighran who owned and operated the remote Seven Emus cattle station in the Northern Territory. 'How far away is it, Tommy?'

Tommy had no idea as to the distance, but he concluded that it would take an hour, or perhaps two, to get there. Heathcock deliberated.

'No,' he said. 'No, it would take too much time. Better get back. If we leave now, we can reach Horse Creek by nightfall.'

The remains were promptly gathered up, placed in the sack and firmly attached onto the back of Bobby.

The sun was setting as the men mounted their horses and turned north-west. It was Monday 10 February 1943.

As the Heathcock party headed home, three miles to the south-east Grady Gaston notched another message on the bark of a tree. It had been eighty days since the crash, maybe eighty-one. The day had brought little in the way of sustenance. Gaston could find only the remains of a dead reptile. As always, his two companions had little enthusiasm for the impending feast.

Arthur Speltz hated snakes. He had never seen one, but he hated them nevertheless. Dyer was no different. Only Gaston had any affinity for reptiles. The daily trips from the shack had nothing to do with seeking a rescue. It was now all about survival. There was only one knife left and one match. Gaston had been saving the match since Christmas. It was to be used only when needed. It might snap like the others, or it might be damp, but to the men it offered hope. It was a potential asset, and Gaston guarded it with his life.

Dead fish were fairly common, but they rested heavy in the gut. Snakes made better eating. Many of them were killed as they lay basking in the sun. Gaston did the killing. None of the men had known such thirst and hunger. A month ago, they could have only guessed at what deprivation would force them to do. The equation was now simple — eat or die. Their bodies were wasting as quickly as their resolve. The small lemon tree next to the shack was a treat with sweet lemon juice, but there was never enough of it. The two things there was no shortage of were the bugs and the feared mosquitoes. The ritual of burying oneself in the sand for temporary relief had not abated since December 2nd.

Late in the afternoon of 10 February 1943, John Dyer lay alone in the bark shack. For five days he had been unable to move. Wracked with fever and badly malnourished, he knew that he was going to die. Gaston and Speltz had left earlier in the day to search for food and water.

Dyer still found it hard to accept that fate had dealt him this predicament. Every night as he slept — or tried to sleep — he kept hoping that he would awake and find that it had all been a dream. He, like the others, had all but given up hope of being rescued. Fate had not only dealt them a bum hand — it had dealt them a death sentence. All that remained were his thoughts. Grady still projected hope and optimism, but Dyer was certain that everyone had long since given up looking. Dyer hated this place, the place where he was going to die. Gaston said he had heard another aircraft, a single engine job, flying over the area sometime in mid-January. They'd have been dead weeks ago if Gaston hadn't found that dead wallaby. The last match had provided their last cooked meal; everything since was raw fish, snakes, lizards and berries. The melon patch in the hut had been their most prized possession.

The daily routine was taking longer as the Americans grew weaker and weaker. Every day they had to go further and further. The search for food was becoming a painful ordeal, even more so when they didn't find any. Gaston and Speltz often settled for a rotting bird or a fish carcass. On this day in February, all they could find were a few cockles. They would have to do. The shack was two hours away and it would soon be dark. They used to be able to walk this distance in an hour, but with every day that they grew weaker, the trip became harder and longer.

Gaston was first into the shack. At first he thought that Dyer was asleep. He called out, but there was no answer.

Dyer was perched upright in the corner of the shack, his head bowed and his hands folded on his lap. He had a piece of bark in his hands, which Gaston carefully removed. Gaston read the text scratched on the bark — 'I lasted till February 10'.

Speltz sat with his hands to his head and he began to weep. Gaston was frozen with grief.

The sun had almost set and soon it would be dark. 'Arthur, you know what we have to do.'

Speltz reluctantly nodded. The men took hold of Dyer and began to remove him from the shack. The beach was only fifty yards away, but the task sapped their energy. They could no longer stand and deliver, only slip and slide. There was a ritual of stopping, resting and starting, until they placed the body face-down on the beach. The three had often discussed this procedure, although they hoped that it would never come to this. John Dyer became the second of *Little Eva*'s crew to lie face-down in the sands of north-west Australia.

CHAPTER EIGHT

'They could still be out there'

NORM CROSSON and Loy Wilson could look back on their ordeal with a sense of relief and a sense of deliverance. They were lost for thirteen days and had nearly died. They could only imagine what it would be like to be missing in that country for a month or even longer. Crosson feared that the men were long dead; he was even more concerned that they might still be alive. The land was merciless and their suffering would be beyond imagination.

After leaving Burketown on December 23rd, Crosson and Wilson were flown to Cairns where they spent Christmas. Two days later they were back at Iron Range. It had been twenty-six days since the mission and a lifetime of experiences. Crosson and Wilson were not alone in their dislike for Iron Range, but after what they had been through, it could almost seem like home. The men of the 90th could not hear the story often enough. Everyone thought that they were lost forever. Crosson's new waistline was the talk of the base. Everyone had called him 'Fats', and now they were calling him 'Slim'. The 200-pound bulk was now down to around 150. Wilson had fared better, but what was most on his mind was the need to get word back home that he was okay.

Wilson was one of the few men of the 90th who had got married before being shipped overseas. He had taken his vows while the group was stationed at Greenville. His wife's name was Arvilla, but for all sorts of reasons he began calling her Billie. Whenever he met anyone he always felt obliged to explain his given name of 'Loy': his father's name was Floyd, and his mother took the three middle letters from his name. While Loy was stationed at Greenville, Billie had found a job as a secretary so they could be together. After Loy was shipped to Willow Run in Michigan, their time together became less frequent and before long he was posted overseas.

As soon as he could after his rescue, Loy sent a telegram to his wife:

DEAREST BILLIE AM FIT AND WELL MY ADDRESS AMIBFO TELL MOM AND GIVE MY LOVE LETTER FOLLOWS.
LOVE
LOY WILSON

Billie had no idea that Loy was even missing, so the telegram caused her concern rather than easing it. But soon a letter arrived and with it the first awareness of his ordeal:

Our crew had to parachute out. I don't know what happened to the other boys but my pilot and I walked for thirteen days without food before being rescued. That was when I was missing in action during December. I am fully recovered now and back to flying. I was sent to hospital in Burketown, Australia. I was hoping to get a brief furlough home but I guess that will have to wait. But then dear, we'll have a lifetime together when we get back.

Crosson was extensively debriefed and was delighted when told that he and Wilson had earned a week's furlough in Sydney. 'What have you heard about the search for the others?' he asked the Squadron Commander.

'We haven't heard a thing yet and nothing from the Australians,' the officer told him. 'We've flown from New Guinea to the coast of Australia as far south as Cairns and down the Gulf of Carpentaria. The ground search was abandoned due to the rain. We've scaled down, but we're still looking. I've been told that the ground search will continue as soon as the ground gets firm again.' He was told that the search for the others was no longer his problem, but he could never forget it. He couldn't get the men out of his mind. He blamed himself for the whole thing, and wished he could do something to help find the men.

Bob Hagarty loved the bush and the challenges it posed. He loved the freedom it offered. He didn't mind being dirty and he enjoyed the company of blacks. Being away from the station and the missus for a while was always welcome. He couldn't understand why anyone, particularly a policeman, could enjoy life in a big city. He had had a gutful of it during his constable days. When he had to go to Brisbane on police business, he felt like a fish out of water. The other police laughed at his demeanour and the long boots he invariably wore. He felt uncomfortable in the headquarters in Roma Street, he didn't like the traffic in the city, and he felt intimidated by the masses of people. Gregory Downs was a different world. Not having a wireless was no big deal and he didn't care that the nearest picture theatre was 200 miles away. He could never get home quickly enough — to swap his cap for his Akubra hat, the blue tunic for his khaki britches, the shoes for his boots, and to get off a train and onto a horse. He enjoyed the regular mounted patrols. The people in the bush treated him like a member of the family. He had spent as much time in the bush as any white man, but this search was something else again.

He had no doubt that this expedition was the most arduous and most frustrating of any that he had been involved in. It was almost a month since he and his three companions had set out from

Burketown, and Hagarty had never ventured so far from home. He estimated that he was now nearly 200 miles from Gregory Downs.

It was obvious that the trip was having a profound effect on both man and beast. Marsh looked gaunt and weary, and Archie and Norman little better. He had no doubt that he looked equally as poorly. Only eight mounts remained and two of them were lame. Hagarty regretted his decision not to proceed to Wollogorang in late January. The search of the area west of Cliffdale Creek and south to Guagudda was hindered by heavy rain. Norman had told him that any tracks that had existed were now washed away forever. Undaunted, Hagarty continued to search the area adjacent to Westmoreland Horse Island in the areas of Lagoon Creek and Buffalo Hole.

On the night of February 3rd, while Marsh and Archie were out searching, Hagarty remained in a makeshift camp, resting with Norman and the horses. It had been twenty-four days since they had left Burketown and he knew that Marsh and the others had serious doubts about the prospects of finding the men. He couldn't believe that the American blokes could be so elusive, and he wondered why they hadn't stayed with the plane. It had been eight weeks since the crash, and even Hagarty would struggle to survive that long. Still, if they knew what they were doing, they could be okay. Hagarty knew that the chances of finding them were becoming remote, but for some reason he felt that there was still hope. The search would continue, but they needed to first stop at Wollogorang Station. There they could get some new mounts, a wash, a feed and a good night's sleep.

Hagarty began to doze, but was awakened at 8.30 pm when Marsh and Archie returned to the camp. 'We searched along the coast up to Guagudda Creek,' said Marsh. 'We went along the saltpans to the north. I didn't see any tracks, but Archie thinks that he did. He thinks that the Yanks have been there, a while ago, and he's got a feeling that they're still around. We covered about forty miles. I thought that we should hurry back, in case you want to start out again in the morning.'

Hagarty was excited by the news, and he rose as quickly as his aching body would allow. 'Archie, what's this about the Yanks?' he asked. 'Do you think that the whitefellas are near the coast somewhere?'

'Yes Boss, I think that they came this way. I saw signs. The tracks are there — almost gone — not blackfellas' tracks, whitemen, near the coast, a long time ago.'

'I always thought that they made for the coast,' said Hagarty. 'If the Yanks are on the coast, we'll find 'em.'

The men knew that there could be no further progress with the search without rest and fresh provisions.

'We'll go to Wollogorang and rest up a bit,' said Hagarty. 'I reckon it's about fifty miles from here — about two days ride to the south-west. How do you feel, Roy? Do you think that the Yanks could still be alive? Could they be holed up somewhere?'

'I dunno, Bob. I'm beginning to think they must be dead,' said Marsh. 'This country is the worst you could come across. Look what it's done to us. We're all buggered. It's either stinking hot or pissing down rain, and those saltpans are crippling the animals. It's only a matter of time before they're all lame, and if we lose our ponies, then we'll all die out here.'

'That's why we have to make for Wollogorang. We can make Branch Creek by tomorrow night and then the station the day after.'

The Wollogorang cattle station was called 'the spirit of the Territory'. The property was bigger than many European countries — nearly 2750 square miles and 1.76 million acres. It had fifty miles of frontage on the Gulf of Carpentaria and lay on either side of the Queensland–Northern Territory border. Like most towns and stations in the area, Wollogorang had a colourful history. The area was first settled in 1883 by the Chisholm family, who had formerly lived in Wollogorang House, near Goldburn in New South Wales. They saw the first cattle arrive in the area, and within forty years over

30 000 head were spread throughout the property. Equally ubiquitous were the Shadforth family who took over the running of the station from the Chisholms in 1895. Old Harry Shadforth was the first of many descendants, both black and white, who lived and ruled on the property. The property was sold to 'Old Man' Anning for £3000. The property was once again sold in 1906 to an English business syndicate, who wanted Wollogorang for the cattle; to them, the land was just wild Australian bush.

A syndicate of North Queensland families reclaimed the bush and the cattle. Nearly forty years later they still owned the cattle, the property and the homestead, which consisted of two upstairs rooms and a storeroom and a dining room below. Bloodwood posts kept the house off the ground and the corrugated iron roof protected the occupants from the elements. It was modest by almost any civilised standards, but being situated in the massive, barren isolation of the Top End, the house was akin to an opulent mansion.

By the outbreak of the war, the station employed forty stockmen. There was also a horse stud containing 600 mostly superb animals. The only communication to the outside world was the fortnightly mail service operating from Burketown. The few visitors who travelled to the station included police officers. The Northern Territory police had granted protection to Wollogorang ever since Old Harry had been speared by an Aboriginal man under a tamarind tree in 1895. There was more trouble until Harry shot dead an Aboriginal and draped his body over a woodheap for three days.

The patrols usually came from the station at Turn Off Lagoon, situated on the Nicholson River twenty miles west of Doomadgee. Patrols from other stations were rare.

On 5 February 1943, a group of black stockmen rode to the homestead to announce the arrival of a police party from Burketown. By the time Hagarty reached the yards, Duncan McLean, the station manager, was there to meet them.

'Jesus! You blokes look like Ned Kelly and Steve Hart.'

The two policemen wore face whiskers mattered with dirt and grime. It may have looked odd, but it was one method of combating the mosquitoes and flies.

'As well as searching for the American airmen, we've been donating blood to Gulf mosquitoes,' said Hagarty.

'Come up to the house and have a drink. Our stockmen will take care of your boys.'

The home-made lemonade was heaven sent. Jack Crowley, the station cook, served it on the homestead's verandah. Hagarty and Marsh sipped it slowly as McLean joined them with another man, who he introduced as Jack Shadforth.

Hagarty recognised the name, but he was surprised that the man was a half-caste Aboriginal, aged about thirty.

'We got word about the crash, the first week of January,' said McLean. 'I sent three groups of blacks to look for them, and Jack here led one of them. Tell them what happened, Jack.'

'About sixteen of us looked in the Settlement Creek area and back along the beach to Lagoon Creek,' said Shadforth. 'We had a real good look along the beach, but didn't find a thing. We were away for about fourteen days. If they made it this far, I reckon we would have found them. The stockmen have been told to keep a look-out for anything unusual.'

Hagarty was surprised that Shadworth spoke like an educated man. 'We tracked them to the coast,' said Hagarty. 'Norman picked up tracks made by shoe leather, just before the last rainfall. I always believed that they made it to the coast. I told Nuss that we should organise a boat and cruise the shore. Where else would they go? If they had a compass they could have made the coast. It's the best place to make for if you're lost.'

'Bob, I hate to say it, but if they made it this far, we would have found them. Jack and I reckon that they never made it out of the Settlement Creek area.'

Hagarty also had his doubts, but he would not be deterred. 'I reckon you're right, they're probably dead. But we've come this far and I want to find them — alive or dead. It's the least we can do after coming this far.'

There was an outpost radio at the homestead and McLean suggested that they send a radiogram to Cloncurry to keep Galligan informed of developments.

Hagarty penned a message and gave it to McLean to send. For the first time he expressed a degree of pessimism:

Inspector of Police,
Cloncurry
Sir arrived Wollogorang Station 5th February. No trace survivors. Tracks obliterated. Please advise if continue search.

Hagarty also thought it prudent to send a wire to Harry Nuss:

Arrived Wollogorang yesterday. No trace survivors. Tracks obliterated. Have advised Inspector.

Hagarty knew that a reply would be forthcoming. As he rested, he thought about what to do next. McLean knew this country as well as anyone. The fact that there had been substantial searches mounted from the station challenged Hagarty's optimism. If he were directed to continue the search, then he would do so and look westward along the coast. But why hadn't these men been seen? This trip had taken its toll on Hagarty and his colleagues. All four men were exhausted and they had mounts and provisions. What chance would four foreigners, walking alone on foot, have in this country? The search was now very much in the Northern Territory and Borroloola was only a couple of days away. Hagarty briefly wondered whether the police there had been brought into the search.

Hagarty did not want to be idle. He organised a new plant of horses and put them in one of the yards, saddles at the ready. Crowley was getting some tucker together. The meal that he'd provided the evening before was the equal of Lennons Hotel, thought Hagarty. Infinitely better than cooking in the bush. Even Marsh seemed rejuvenated by the hospitality. 'Bob, if you want to carry on, I'm with you. So are Norman and Archie. I've gotta' tell you that I think they're gone, but I'm with you. At least the area westwards up to the coast is a lot better than the saltpans and bush we've come through. I do feel sorry for those poor buggers.'

Harry Nuss was by now accustomed to waiting. Ever since this bloody mess started he had been a virtual observer waiting and responding. It had been nearly four weeks since the Hagarty group had left Burketown. It would be just his luck if something had happened to them.

When the Hagarty wire arrived in Burketown, Nuss was pleased, first, they were okay and, second, if the search was to be discontinued, it would be Galligan's decision. Nuss was relived. He did not relish that responsibility.

While awaiting the inevitable response from Nuss and Galligan, Marsh, Hagarty, Norman and Archie were kept busy. At least the horses were being rested and some of them might be fit enough to continue the trek. The gear was badly worn after weeks in the scrub, and the rain and salt water had perished much of the leather. Marsh and Archie greased the surfaces, to good effect. They were used to making things do; in the bush you had to be resourceful. Hagarty made repeated attempts to reach Constable Chapman at the Lawn Hill station, about two hundred miles to the south-west, but was unsuccessful. He wanted to try Borroloola — they were more likely to have heard something — but the station was under the jurisdiction

MU23 46 GOVT=WMU WASHINGTON DC 29 210P

STANLEY P SELTZ= ★ ☆

:505 ALBERTLEA AVE

1943 MAY 29 PM 1 25

:THE SECRETARY OF WAR DESIRES THAT I TENDER HIS DEEP SYMPATHY TO YOU IN THE LOSS OF YOUR BROTHER SECOND LIEUTENANT ARTHUR N SPELTZ PREVIOUSLY REPORTED MISSING IN ACTION REPORT JUST RECEIVED STATES THAT HE DIED ON FEBRUARY TWENTY FOUR IN SOUTHWEST PACIFIC AREA LETTER FOLLOWS=

:ULIO THE ADJUTANT GENERAL.

A telegram from Western Union confirms the worst to the Speltz family.

Staff Sergeant Loy L. Wilson

'Wild Man' Grady Gaston in front of the Borroloola Police Station, May 1943.

Gaston, with the luxury of a Lucky Strike cigarette, recounts his ordeal to an American officer and stenographer.

LT. A. N. SPELTZ.
321st Sqd - 90th Bomb &
A.P.O - 932 - % Postmaster
San Francisco, Calif.
Nov 3 - 1942

Dear Mom:

I wrote you a V-mail also today so you can compare the time of arrival. I am enclosing a check for which you can buy my christmas presents & present them for me. You know what they all need & want the most. Get as follows:

Billy - 10⁰⁰   You can let me know
Betty - 10⁰⁰   what you got them.
Lauretta - 10⁰⁰
Stan   5⁰⁰
Ang   5⁰⁰
Mary   5⁰⁰
       # 45⁰⁰

You can get them something either one big thing or two or so smaller articles. I am sending this early so you will get it soon enough. Your gift will come from elsewhere.

Did you get the snapshots as yet? Our mail service is not bad, but will be delayed now a few days due to forwarding address.

Am enclosing a few sea shells & native beads we found on some Islands enroute & also the check. thought the beads would look strange & different to you. they just lay on the ocean shore at these places & just have to pick them up. The people don't wear any clothes to speak of at some of the South Sea islands. The Cathol missions & nuns are getting them to do so now. We ate with some back in the woods & it was fun. they all sit on the floor in their grass huts. We had Coconut milk, Coconut, Papaya fruit & alot of other stuff I didn't care to much for. They eat raw fish & when they passed that arou

( ) (2nd Letter from APO-932)

AG 201 Speltz, Arthur N.   WASHINGTON
       (5-27-43) PC-N 147082

                                        5 June, 1943   JUL 15 1943

       Mrs. Laura Speltz,
            406 Water Street,
               Albert Lea, Minnesota.

Dear Mrs. Speltz:

            It grieves me that it is necessary to inform you
of the death of your son, Second Lieutenant Arthur N. Speltz,
0-727,935, Air Corps. My notification telegram was sent to
his brother, Mr. Stanley P. Speltz, who was designated by him
as the emergency addressee.

            A casualty report received in this office, from the
Commanding General of the Southwest Pacific Area, states that
your son, who was previously reported "missing in action," since
1 December, 1942, died on 24 February, 1943. This determination
was reached by military authorities after a thorough investiga-
tion into his case. I regret that the report did not state the
date and place of burial.

            These reports are of necessity brief due to the
conditions of war under which they are made. However, should
additional information be received in this office, please be
assured that it will be sent to you immediately. An information
bulletin is inclosed for your help and guidance.

            May the thought that his supreme sacrifice was made in
the grim struggle to maintain the freedom of his country be of
some solace to you.

            I extend my deepest sympathy in your great loss.

                              Sincerely yours,

                              J. A. ULIO
                              Major General,
                              The Adjutant General.

1 Incl.

Lieut. Arthur Speltz Dies In Wilds Of Australia After Forced Landing Of Bomber

Staff Sergeant Gaston, Sole Survivor, Tells of Being Lost† For 141 Days; Four of Survivors Ate Snakes, Fish and Crocodiles and Other Meat; Speltz Died on February 24

By VERN HAUGLAND

LIEUTENANT ARTHUR SPELTZ

Allied headquarters in Australia, May 25—AP—Staff Sergeant Grady Gaston of Frisco City, Ala., is recovering in an army hospital from near starvation after being lost 141 days in wild gulf country in northern Australia and watching three of his companions perish.

Gaston and five others survived the forced landing of their Liberator heavy bomber in the northern part of the Commonwealth after returning from a raid on a Japanese base in December.

Two of the survivors, Capt. Norman Crosson, Cincinnati, and Sergeant Loy Wilson were found by searchers 13 days after the forced landing. (The dispatch did not name the other three survivors or indicate how they were rescued.)

Gaston and Co-pilot Lieut. Arthur Speltz, Albert Lea, Minn.; Bombardier Lieut. John Dyer, Boston and Navigator Lieut. Dale Grimes, Boston, remained lost during the days of wandering.

Gaston said the four shot a steer on the third day.

The first to die was Grimes, who was drowned while attempting to cross a stream to reach a passion fruit vine. "I tried to rescue him," said Gaston, "but I was too weak. We could only watch him as he was swept out to sea."

Late in December, Gaston and his two remaining companions decided to make camp and wait in hopes a searching party would find them.

They started a small melon patch which, with snakes, occasional fish and crocodile meat, provided their only food. Mosquitoes and other insects sapped their strength nightly.

Gaston alone, wandered aimlessly, drinking water from stagnant holes where crocodiles wallowed and catching sand crabs with his bare hands.

Gaston says: "We lived on snakes, fish and crocodiles, which we had to eat raw because we had no matches to light fires," Gaston related.

"By early February my weight dropped from 168 to 100 pounds.

"On February 10 we decided to make for a nearby waterhole. Dyer collapsed. We went on to get water for him, but when we returned he was dead.

"On Feb. 24, Speltz died in his sleep. From then on, I lost track of time. Some days I found nothing to eat. Once I fought off a pack of dingoes (wild dogs) which had killed a cow, so I could get some meat.

"I had nearly given up the fight when some black boys found me and led me to a white man who fed me. After several days we went back, got the bodies of Dyer and Speltz and took them to a cemetery. Then I was flown to the hospital."

The Albert Lea newspaper reveals the fate of a local hero.

Norman Crosson photographed in 1958.

The only known photo of Jack Keighran, after the war.

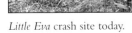

Little Eva crash site today.

In memory of the crew of the American
B24D Liberator No 12762 'Little Eva'
321st Squadron 90th Bomb Group
U.S.A.F. which crashed near
Moonlight Creek on 2nd December 1942

1st Lt. Norman R. CROSSAN

2nd Lt. Arthur N. SPELTZ

2nd Lt. Dale V. GRIMES

2nd Lt. John D. DYER

S/Sgt. James B. HILTON

S/Sgt. Grady B. GASTON

S/Sgt. Charles B. WORKMAN Jr

Sgt. Edward J. McKEEN

Sgt. Loy L. WILSON

Cpl. John GEYDOS Jr

Recently erected memorial in Doomadgee, northwest Queensland, to the crew of *Little Eva*. Crosson's name is misspelled.

of Alice Springs. It was prudent not to instigate any contact; that was up to Galligan.

Hagarty spent time drawing a proper sketch of the plane. He had made detailed notes, but now he had the time and the facilities to make an accurate representation. He had always enjoyed drawing and spent many an hour sketching at Gregory Downs. A drawing would enhance his report, which would be the first thing that Galligan asked for. It was mid-morning on February 6th when Duncan McLean called him over to the big house. 'Bob, there's a radiogram coming in for you. I think it's from Cloncurry. We're jotting it down for you now.'

The wire was indeed from Galligan:

Constable Hagarty
Wollogorang Radio (8QX)
You may discontinue search. Constable Marsh to return to Burketown.
Please take up with Chapman party at Lawn Hill.

The response did not surprise Hagarty, but it left him with a feeling of bitter disappointment. The trek had long since ceased to be just a police search; it had become deeply personal. Whatever chance the Americans had of being found had now vanished and he now knew that he would never find them.

'Roy, it's over. The search is finished. Galligan has called it off. You and Archie are to return to Burketown. I've been ordered to go to Lawn Hill — God knows why.'

'It's probably got something to do with cattle,' said Marsh. 'I hear that John Chapman has some trouble with illegal cattle dipping.'

'Well, tell the boys that we leave in the morning. We can ride part of the way together.'

The police party left at 8.30 am the following day. The fact that they were heading south-east instead of north-west created a sombre mood. Hagarty wanted to make Westmoreland Station — another remote outback property, situated about thirty miles from Wollogorang — by dark. After twelve hours riding they arrived, and Hagarty was relieved to find that Tom Terry was still in residence. They had met months before while on mounted patrol and Hagarty wanted to test the friendship by procuring some horses, at least five more. The men were billeted for the night and were back in the saddle again by 7.30 the next morning. It was another arduous day, twenty miles to Stratton's Creek. The next day the party made thirty-two miles, to Turn Off Lagoons. George Burns was another station owner who had learned to live with the harshness of the land and the isolation. Hagarty had pushed the others hard that day. He wanted to talk to Burns about a jacket that Burns was purported to have found.

It was after 8.00pm when they arrived. They were escorted to the house by a large party of blacks, for this was something interesting; nothing much ever happened here and visitors were big news.

There was time for a cup of tea, a feed and a smoke before Hagarty told Burns about Inspector Galligan in Cloncurry calling off the search for the American aviators.

'I'm interested as to how you came about the jacket. Where did you find it? Can you give us a look at it?'

'We heard about the crash at Christmas time,' said Burns. 'I started a search with three blacks and went to Point Parker. We met a party of blacks from Mornington Island, who had found tracks near Doomadgee Creek. We went back with them, found some more tracks, and followed them as far as Cliffdale Creek. The tracks were fairly recent; could have been a week old. That's where we found the jacket. It was floating in the water. I'd bet that the Yank took it off in order to get across. Jesus, it was wet at the time, simply pissing down. We'd been out for thirteen days and the horses were knocked up. We had to give it up.'

Hagarty was surprised at the condition of the jacket. It was superbly made and showed few signs of wear. Somewhat like a lumber jacket, it had a zipper up the front and two breast pockets. On the right breast pocket, the name J. B. Hilton was clearly visible.

'I'll bet that Hilton is one of the men missing,' said Burns. 'I reckon that they made it to Cliffdale Creek, but never made it out. The crocs probably got them. I reckon that this jacket is all you're going to find. They're goners for sure. You can forget the coast or the Robinson — they never made it that far. They never crossed Cliffdale Creek.'

'I'm not so sure,' said Hagarty. 'Anyway, we'll have to take the jacket back to Burketown as evidence.'

Hagarty did not have to spend the next few days in the saddle after all. Chapman sent word that he and Joe Sammon were coming by car to give him a lift back to Lawn Hill. They would arrive in the morning with some fresh clothes.

Hagarty was right — the new case was a routine affair involving local cattle dipping. He doubted that his participation had even been necessary, but at least he got a lift home. It was March 10th when Hagarty finally returned to Alice and the kids at Gregory Downs. He had been away for nearly two months, the longest that he had ever been away from his family.

Marsh, Archie and Norman arrived at Burketown at 3 pm on February 13th. Nuss was there to greet them. He was relieved that the affair was at last over. It may not have had a happy ending, but it was over. Harry Nuss took the jacket from Marsh and placed it with the five parachutes that had been kept at the back of the station. He was going to keep them there until someone claimed them, or until Galligan told him otherwise.

Galligan sent a telegram to Commissioner Carroll on February 25th:

I have the honour to report that since my last telegram inquiries have been continued. But no trace of the remaining four members of the crew has been found. The search has been discontinued.

Marsh wrote his report for Galligan on February 17th. He specu-
lated about the fate of the Americans. Clearly, he had not forgotten
the conversation with George Burns:

> *About the four survivors, who were walking along the coast in a westerly
> direction, I am of the opinion that they either perished, or tried to swim
> Cliffdale Creek and were either taken by sharks or alligators. The other
> search parties would have found their tracks, because they were there before
> very much rain had fallen, but they were of the opinion that they did not go
> west of Cliffdale Creek.*

Hagarty wrote his report on March 21st. Like Marsh, he wrote
what he believed his superiors wanted to read:

> *It is possible that these men were taken by alligators in Cliffdale Creek, or
> creeks further west, as these creeks abound in saurian of this kind and are
> not man-shy. It is also possible that the men could have wandered south-
> wards into thick coastal scrub and perished, although search of country,
> south, west, north and east, where the last tracks were seen failed to reveal
> any trace of them.*
>
> *It is my opinion that the men perished in the thick coastal scrub south of
> Cliffdale or Guagudda and their skeletons may possibly be chanced upon
> by musterers from Turn Off Lagoons or Westmoreland Station at a future
> date.*
>
> *A ground party of approximately forty men consisting of members of the
> V.D.C. of this district and members of local Military camps had
> endeavoured with the aid of an aeroplane to locate the crashed plane, but
> failed to do so, and as far as I am aware they made no attempt to locate the
> four men who were heading west from the crashed plane.*
>
> *On February 5th 1943, I received a reply, by Radiogram from my
> Inspector, at Wollogorang, that the search may be discontinued and on Feb-
> ruary 6th the party commenced return journey.*
>
> *I attach hereto a rough sketch of the crashed plane.*

Hagarty asked Alice to read the report before he posted it to Galligan. It was the longest and most important he had ever written.

'Do you really think that this is what happened?' asked Alice.

'I have many doubts, but I can hardly tell Galligan that he was wrong in calling off the search. I just wish that we had had a couple more days to look for them. I suppose that they're long gone, but there's just something that's bothering me.'

'Why did you write about the search by the army?' asked Alice. 'What's that got to do with you and Roy?'

'Because no one has found them, or found the bodies. I can't believe that they wouldn't have tried to stay in the open. They made for the coast, that's for sure, and no one has searched the coast properly. I told them at Christmas to get a boat and have a look, but they wouldn't listen. They could still be out there waiting for somebody to find them. I'm worried, Alice, that I may have let them down. I just don't think that this thing is over.'

CHAPTER NINE

'I'm gonna get outta this place'

ARTHUR SPELTZ had long since ceased to be an authority figure to Gaston, for the ordeal had produced a common bond, devoid of rank or seniority. The health of Speltz had been variable since the trek began. His feet had swollen and blistered, but still he kept walking. Since the death of Dyer, Speltz had lost focus and seemed resigned to his fate. Gaston, as always, was prepared to do anything to survive. The difference between he and the others was his willingness to eat anything that would supply sustenance. One day in February, Gaston saw a snake slipping away towards the foliage. He promptly killed the reptile with a rock and returned to the shack, snake in hand. His entrance startled Speltz, who still hated and feared anything that crawled.

'Arthur, look what I've found. It's fresh and fat. I killed it near the beach, near the big tree. It must have been sunning itself.'

Gaston pointed the reptile towards Speltz, who could only grimace and turn his head away in disgust. He soon became a mute witness to the spectacle of Gaston dissecting and skinning the reptile.

'You've got to eat something, Arthur. It's not bad. You've got to chew it quickly and swallow. Just watch me.'

Gaston proceeded to tear a piece of flesh from the snake and place it in his mouth.

'You wanna' try some?'

Speltz shook his head, but Gaston was not deterred. 'I'll save you some in case you change your mind. I'll leave it over here.' Speltz could only dry retch.

Gaston admired the young lieutenant. It had been a week since Dyer died and Gaston had offered to continue the search for food and water, but Speltz insisted that he do his share. The daily jaunts for supplies continued, but they did not venture east of the hut towards the sea. Neither wanted to see the body of John Dyer, which lay less than fifty yards from the hut. The two men wished that it were fifty miles. Speltz's journeys from the shack were as laborious as they were torturous. Arthur often told Gaston not to worry if he was not back until late. 'Sometimes the tide is up and the creek is too wide to cross,' he would say. 'I'll have to wait until the water drops. Don't worry. I'll come back when I can.'

Gaston remembered the words, but on February 20th it was different. Arthur had not returned by nightfall, and, worse, it was raining. Gaston was concerned and that night he did not sleep well. As soon as it was daylight, Gaston scanned the area for any sign of his buddy. He yearned to see the emaciated and crouched figure of Speltz approaching the shack with a handful of passionfruit or berries. At least they did not have to worry about water. The heavy rain had filled up the customised life vests, two of which still served as crude water containers. Gaston hoped that Speltz was still waiting for the tide to subside, or that he had gone further inland, but by noon he could wait no longer.

He left the shack and walked in the direction that Speltz had taken. The sun disappeared and the rain returned, fierce and heavy. It drove the stooping, struggling Gaston back towards the shack. The rain eventually began to ease, but Gaston's anxiety did not. He gazed along the banks of the creek, dreading the thought of finding Arthur lying face down in the water. At 2.00 pm the rain stopped. Gaston was about to cross the creek to search on the other bank when he saw a figure on the sand near the water's edge. It was Speltz. There was no movement. 'Please, don't let him be dead,' Gaston prayed. Suddenly Gaston heard a sound and saw Speltz raise his right arm as if to wave, and Gaston rushed to his buddy as quickly as his weak limbs would allow.

'Grady, thank God you've come. I can't move. I've been lying here for hours. Lying in the rain. I prayed you would come. Thank God! Can you help me up?'

'Take it easy, Arthur. I'm here. Give me your arm. I'll help you up.'

'I'm scared, Grady. I'm scared of dyin'.'

'Nobody's goin' to die. I'll get you up and take you home. A little rest and you'll be as good as new.'

The rain had ceased, but there was a strong wind and Speltz could not maintain his balance. He walked and then fell. Gaston helped as much as he could, but the strong wind was knocking them both down. Gaston could see the shack. It was only eighty feet or so away, but it became a marathon. He placed Speltz on his back and grasped him under the armpits. Yard by yard, he dragged him then stopped, dragged him then stopped. He had little energy and it became difficult to breathe.

'Leave me, Grady, and save yourself. I don't think I can go on,' said Speltz.

'Don't talk crazy,' replied Gaston. 'We can make it; we're nearly home; just a few more yards.'

Gaston could see that Speltz was in a bad way. He was skeletal with no colour. His ankles and legs were grotesquely swollen and it was obvious that he had a fever. The young officer was dying.

The shack became a sanctuary. Getting Speltz propped up into a corner was physically arduous. 'Arthur, I'll get you a melon — would you like a melon? I'll get you some water as well. Stay here, I'll be back. Are you okay?'

Speltz was going nowhere. He sensed that he would never move again. Gaston returned with some bush fruit and Arthur had his first meal in two days.

'Grady, what day is this? What's the date? Is it February twenty something?'

'February 23rd, I think,' said Gaston.

'I feel a lot better. Thanks, Grady, for coming to get me. Thanks for the melons.'

That night, the rain eased to a trickle. The men could hear the drops hitting the bark roof. There were plenty of leaks and the rain had cooled things.

Gaston could not remember Speltz being so voluble. He talked about Albert Lea and the family company, and it was clear that he was devoted to his mother, his brother and his three sisters. His father had died in 1932. Speltz's main concern was that his family would be worrying about him.

Gaston's background could not have been more different. He had a sister, but his father was no businessman, having worked the fields all of his life. Farm life was tough during the depression: 'Never leave anything on your plate; always eat what you've got,' he would tell his son. It was not until Grady joined the army that he saw anything other than Frisco City and that he consistently had three square meals a day.

'Grady, you can call me Tony if you want to, but I want you to promise me something. If I don't make it out of here I want you to write to my folks. Tell them I was thinking about them — tell them that I did my duty.'

'You can write to 'em yourself,' said Gaston. 'We'll both get out of here. We gotta' keep hoping. Remember what Dale used to say about not giving up. If he was here now, he would tell you the same thing.'

'Just promise me you'll write to my folks.'

'Okay, just try to get some sleep. I'll set out early in the morning to look for some more food.'

Gaston enjoyed the nights more than the days. It was cooler, and at high tide he could hear the breakers on the beach. Mosquitoes and bugs aside, it was more peaceful, and sleep became a temporary respite from the ever-prevailing nightmare. The men slept as often and as late as they could. Once unconscious, they felt no pain — the demons could be held at bay for a few hours.

On the night of February 23rd, Gaston was sound asleep when something woke him. He sat up and saw that Speltz was grasping his wrist and then his hand. Speltz tried to sit up and talk, but was unable to. He squeezed Gaston's hand harder and then Gaston heard a moan. 'Arthur, what's the matter? Are you okay?'

Still there was no sound. Speltz managed to move a little and Gaston tried to help him. Speltz lifted his body up a little and then fell into Gaston's lap. Nobody moved; nobody made a sound.

Sometime in the early hours of 24 February 1943, a young man from Minnesota died in the arms of a boy from Alabama, in a paperbark hut in north-eastern Australia.

Gaston did not often cry. He came from tough stock. Nevertheless, that night and that morning, in the Australian wilderness, he wept uncontrollably. He wept for his buddies; he wept for himself. His worst fear had been realised. He was now alone. For a moment he wished that he too was dead, but then he was glad he was alive. He knew what had to be done.

Moving Speltz from the shack was tough enough, but to drag him to the beach where Dyer still lay seemed an insurmountable task. It was only fifty yards, but Gaston could do only a yard at a time. What should have taken a few minutes took a day — the hardest day of his life. There were more tears, and there were screams of anguish and torment. There was no one to listen, and he felt like he was the only person left in the world.

At last Gaston placed Speltz on his face next to the remains of John Dyer. 'Arthur, I'm sorry this had to happen to you. You were the best of all of us. You were a good man. God bless you, Arthur. Rest in peace.'

Gaston walked and crawled back to the shack. It was miserable haunt, but it was the only refuge he had. He didn't want to stay out in the open. He sat in the corner and gazed at the graffiti on the walls: Dyer's scrawls, Grimes' initials, Speltz's crucifix and the seemingly endless date scrawlings. It was time for another day, another mark. He decided to let it wait a while. He thought back to how they had spent Christmas in this place, when the situation was dangerous but not desperate. He was thankful that they did not know then what was in store for them — that in a few weeks all except one would be dead. The shack was small, but now it seemed like an auditorium. Gaston could feel and almost hear the ghosts. He wanted to leave, but there was nowhere to go. Was he going to die there, just like his buddies? Gaston drew upon his resolve. He wasn't going to die — not today — he was going to make it. He said it out aloud. 'I'm gonna' get outta' this place. I want to get back to Frisco City and see my family. I want to have a normal life. I'm going to meet a girl. I'm going to own an automobile.'

Gaston not only wanted to survive; he wanted to live to tell what happened here — to tell everybody about the crew of *Little Eva*. Gaston made another silent pledge. His buddies would not lie and rot in this place. He was going to make sure that they all went home.

Gaston knew that he had to continue the daily treks for food and water. As well as being necessary for survival, it kept him occupied and took his mind off things. It did not get any easier: the creeks seemed to be further away; the hills seemed higher. He rued the day that they had lost their hunting knife. Dyer had blamed Speltz and Speltz had blamed Dyer. It didn't matter. The knife was lost — probably in a creek. One day Gaston found an old spearhead and a rotting sheath at the base of a tree. The handle was missing, but the head still had an edge. It must have been here for years, Gaston thought. A native must have left it here — an Aboriginal. He had seen them near the base at Iron Range, but had had nothing to do with them. They seemed withdrawn and aloof. He had been told that they were no trouble, and that was okay by him; the last thing he wanted was to have them down on him.

Gaston was no longer capable of hunting for food. His gaunt and undernourished body did not possess the necessary vigour. He was no longer a predator; he was now a scavenger. Water could only be taken from the stinking, stagnant holes that he had previously avoided, but it did not seem to matter anymore. The need to quench his thirst became overwhelming. Food was another story; scraps and remains were few and the berries had long since been plucked. The vine on the shack had withered and died. He no longer had the strength to venture far from the shack. Sand crabs were plentiful but elusive. He caught the odd one or two on the beach and gutted them with the spearhead. As always, the meals were raw — chew quickly and swallow. Sometimes it was difficult to digest the portions; he often gagged and threw up. The worst part was the killing of the creatures. The spearhead often slipped and cut his hands, which was as painful as it was frustrating. Gaston left the blade in the shack and further attempts to catch sand crabs depended on his level of hunger. He was no longer quick enough to corner them on the beach; instead he searched for their nesting place — a burrow or a hole. The only way to feast was to get on his knees and reach into the opening and grab the little bastards. Then he would place them on a rock and hit them with another rock. Sometimes a crab would grip his finger with its pincers, and the pain would be so intense that he'd shake his wrist until the crab relinquished its grip and ran off. Once he got them on to a rock face, he'd pummel them with a vengeance, often striking his own fingers in the process. How it hurt. He'd use both hands until they were bloody, tearing off the legs and eating them not just as a source of sustenance but also an outlet for his rage. He dreaded the time of day when he did battle with the crabs. He cried tears and he cried out in pain, but then, just like every other source of food, the crabs vanished.

Nobody knows when Jack Keighran came to Seven Emus. Legend suggests that he arrived some time after the Great War, around 1919. He was one of the first white men to arrive in the area since Leichhardt. Jack came from the Queensland country town of Bundaberg. He was almost born in the saddle and had started life as a jackaroo at the age of ten. Cattle were his life. He may have served in the First War, but no one knows for sure. His age was also a mystery. Years later his family reckoned that he was born around 1897. Whatever his age, Jack was a young man when he came to Seven Emus. The war had been good to the cattle people, and unlike the thousands of young men who came back from the war and ventured north, south or east to the big cities, in search of fame and fortune, Jack headed west — as far west as he could go.

There were no claims necessary to be made on outback land in those days. You simply took what you wanted and fenced it. The name of Seven Emus came from the Leichhardt expedition. Jack found an old shack and persuaded a few Aboriginals to help him. He began to build his business and his future, and by the 1930s the Seven Emus property encompassed 750 square miles. The shack had become a homestead. It was no mansion, but it had a timber floor and a tin roof. Jack had six Aboriginal stockmen and 500 head of cattle. It was a constant challenge to keep the cattle in the paddocks and to keep healthy enough to drive them to Cloncurry; from there, they would then be sold and processed for consumption in the big towns.

Jack Keighran's world was a unique one. His home was in one of the most isolated areas of the continent. There were no neighbours for miles and the nearest town was Borroloola, which was three days ride away. Jack knew about privation and he was forced to stock essentials like grain, food and tobacco. During the wet season, the property often became flood-bound and it could stay that way for weeks or months. The creeks provided water, and kerosene provided the glow necessary for Jack to read his books, which he obtained from the well-stocked library in Borroloola. He was religious, but not overtly so. He spoke to his Aboriginal workers about the Lord, but never professed to be a missionary.

In the big cities, most white Australians seldom saw a black. Where Jack Keighran came from you seldom saw a white. His relationship with the blacks was one of mutual need and respect. Seven Emus could not function without the stockmen and Jack had the best, like Willie Shadforth, Dinnie McDinney and Strike-a-Light. They worked hard and they were loyal. Jack paid them £3 a week. It was an impressive wage for anyone at that time, black or white. In 1937, he took an Aboriginal woman called Jennie into his house. A year later, Jack became the father of a son he called John. In 1939, a second son, Max, was born.

Seven Emus had almost no contact with the outside world. It was only from his visits to Borroloola that Jack knew about the outbreak of the war in Europe. The war was of little interest to him. He could live in blissful isolation, as he was too old to enlist. Even if he had been the right age, his role as a cattleman gave him an exemption from conscription. It came as no surprise when the demand for beef escalated and the drives to Cloncurry became more frequent and involved larger herds.

The war in Europe might be of no concern, but the Japanese menace was another matter. In early 1942, the Australian public was becoming traumatised by the ever approaching Japanese hordes. The news that Jack heard about the war in the Pacific was all bad.

The Japanese were getting closer. When they bombed Darwin in February, fear turned into panic. The people who lived in the Top End expected that a Japanese invasion was imminent. The tension was eased with news about the arrival of some American forces, but Jack knew that they were in the big cities and would be of no help where he was.

If the Japs came to Seven Emus, there would be nothing waiting for them. Jack vowed to burn the house down, destroy his stores and slaughter the stock. He was going to leave Seven Emus with nothing but Jennie and the two boys.

Jack knew that it would do no good to worry about invasion and its consequences. He had enough to worry about with Seven Emus. By 1942, it was becoming increasingly difficult to handle, because the demand for stock and beef was escalating.

The mustering treks were now constant. Young John often accompanied his father on trips to search for stray stock and fix broken fences, although he never went on the longer journeys. The property extended all the way to the coast. It took a man several days to ride the boundaries of Seven Emus and Jack was often away for days at a time. He often left the homestead with several stockmen and a plant of horses, but he seldom rode the boundary all the way to the coast. He left that to his stockmen, his 'boys'.

Once at the coast, it was at least a day's ride back home. In 1930, Jack built a paperbark hut near the beach to be used as overnight accommodation by boundary riders. It was also useful to store saddles and supplies when mustering in the area. It was nothing fancy, but it worked well enough as a refuge from the sun, wind and rain.

In late 1942, the rains were heavier than normal and nobody from Seven Emus mustered along the coast for three months. It was mid-April of the following year before riders from the station were able to venture back to the area. There was much work to be done and Jack decided to go along and inspect the boundaries. On April

18th, he rode out of Seven Emus with three stockmen and a plant of ten horses. He told Jennie not to worry; he could be gone for as long as a week.

One thing that Grady Gaston was determined to do was to keep an accurate record of the time. The thin bark of the shack's wall was covered with scrawls and a makeshift calendar. Every day when the sun came up, Gaston notched another day on the wall. One hundred and ten; one hundred and twenty and then it was one hundred and thirty-two. It was over four months since the crash and three months since they had arrived at the hut. It must now be mid-April, Gaston thought. The world and the war had passed him by. He worried about his mother. She would have received the telegram by now and would think that he was dead. How he wished he could get word to her that he was alive — at least for the moment, anyway.

The 90th Bomb Group was continuing to prosecute the war. The searches for Arthur Speltz and his men had long since been abandoned. The group had plenty to worry about. Since December 1942, ten aircraft and 140 men had been lost. The Allied push through New Guinea and in the south-west Pacific meant that forces were constantly being redeployed — always to the north.

Two squadrons from the 90th moved from Iron Range in late January 1943. Colonel Ralph Koon and an advanced echelon left North Queensland to set up operations in New Guinea. The 320th and 321st squadrons flew to their new base in late January and the 319th Squadron was posted to Darwin. The 400th Squadron remained at Iron Range until March. The group had suffered serious losses while based in Australia. However, the Americans were claiming the destruction of twenty-nine Japanese surface ships and ninety-one enemy aircraft.

On a global scale, the fortunes of war were turning in favour of the

Allies. The conflict in the Atlantic was being won in a battle of attrition. The Germans were being forced out of Tunisia and the Wehrmacht in Russia was facing resurgent Russian armies after the disaster in Stalingrad. The war in the Pacific was also going badly for the Japanese. The savage land, sea and air battles for the island of Guadalcanal had favoured the Americans. The Japanese had evacuated the island in February 1943. There were to be no more conquests for the Rising Sun. The overwhelming might of American forces and the nation's industrial capacity meant that there could be only one winner. By April 1943, the road to Tokyo was already being mapped out.

The scale of the war was vast, but it could be personal as well. On 4 April 1943, a B-24D Liberator from the 514th Squadron, 376th Bomb Group, left Benina in Libya for a bombing raid over Naples. *Lady Be Good*, under the command of Lieutenant William J. Hatton, became lost on the return flight over the Mediterranean and disappeared into the vastness of the Libyan Desert. Sixteen years later, a British oil exploration crew found the wreck of the aircraft 440 miles south-east of Benghazi. The remains of six of the crew were subsequently found. A diary was recovered from the remains of the co-pilot, Second Lieutenant Robert F. Toner, which revealed that the ship had run out of petrol. The crew had bailed out and met back at the wreck, and decided to attempt to walk back to civilisation. The ordeal was not dissimilar to that of Norman Crosson's crew, except that Hatton's crew did not suffer as long. Toner's diary revealed that the men had died within days of their aircraft going down. All perished in the neutral sands of the Libyan Desert.

Gaston's forays from the hut were becoming infrequent. He often wanted to stay indoors and not venture out. He knew that if he did not search for food he would become incapacitated and would soon die. Every day he forced himself to undertake the increasingly difficult and exhausting routine of finding food and water. He could no longer walk over the hills and cross the rivers. Food had to be found in close proximity to the hut. The recent rains had revived the passion-fruit vines and Gaston revelled in a modest feast.

Gaston had always loved dogs. There were always plenty of them back on the farm. Whether hunting or playing, dogs were Grady's best friends. But the dogs in the Australian bush didn't look like house dogs; they looked a little like wolves or coyotes. One thing for sure, they did not seem friendly. He had seen some of them back at the base with the young Aboriginal boys. In the last week or so he had noticed these bush dogs coming closer and closer to the hut. They did not seem to be frightened, so he screamed at them and wielded a stick. They never took a backwards step and Gaston became frightened; two of them were now starting to follow him as he made his daily treks for food and water. They came close enough to snap at his heels. Gaston lurched at them, yelling as loudly as he could. They retreated and then came at a rush towards him, growling and snarling. 'Get outta here, you bastards — git!' Gaston walked backwards towards the shack. He hadn't been as scared since that day at the river. He knew that if they took to him, he could not fight them off; he was too weak, there were days when he couldn't walk at all, so he crawled, on all fours, just like an animal.

From that day on, Gaston never left the hut without a stick. He was not sure how well he could wield it, but he could scare them a little. The days passed. Gaston figured it to be around mid-April. He could check for sure if he used the calendar on the hut wall, but he didn't have the patience. What did it matter if it was April 15th or 16th. He was still stuck in this terrible, forlorn place. He knew that he was dying, and wondered how much longer it would take before he was unable to move.

Uncle Sam's rags were holding up a lot better than Gaston's body. It was difficult for Gaston to walk without losing his pants. The belt had run out of holes. He had gone through at least four hole positions. He was forever pulling up his pants. His teeth were also getting loose. That was all he needed — his teeth to start falling out. He had not seen a reflection of himself since the crash, which was okay by him, but he knew he must look a fright. He could feel a bushy beard and shoulder-length hair. The hair was like straw; it was filthy and matted. But his appearance was the least of his worries. He had never felt so hungry. Today he would have to find some food; anything would do.

The dogs were not around on this day. He looked in all directions, but they had gone. He thanked God for that. The sun was harsh and the ground dry. It was tough to walk. His boots were okay, but the socks had rotted away. His heals were blistered. No need to rush. Jesus! I wish I had a cigarette. Being hungry is bad enough, but a cigarette. That's what I really miss. Shoot! He remembered that he had left a carton back at the base, but who would have thought to bring it along. The mission was only going to last a few hours. Jesus, I wish I had just one Lucky, he thought.

Suddenly he heard a noise like a dogfight. There was barking and growling and Gaston soon saw what was going on. The dogs had not gone away. They were in front of him about thirty yards away, tearing at the flesh of a small bullock that they had obviously killed. They didn't seem to notice him; they were too preoccupied. Gaston counted six of them. The meat was fresh; the dogs were probably as ravenous as he was.

Gaston pondered what to do. Maybe, it would be better if he did nothing. The dogs might leave something and he could always come back later. But his need for food was too strong. He was no different to the dogs — it was eat or die. Gaston took a deep breath and rushed the animals, shouting and waving his stick. They momentarily scattered, and Gaston fell on top of the carcass, his one thought to try and get a scrap or two. He felt a sharp pain on his left ankle. One of the dogs had him by the shin and another snapped at his shoulder. Gaston screamed. He instinctively grabbed at a limb, the better part of a leg, and tore it from the cow. He turned around and swung it at the dog, hitting both the animal and his ankle. The dog let go of him and grimacing in pain Gaston began to crawl away. The dogs had no further interest in him and resumed their feast. Gaston stumbled his way back to the hut, looking around from time to time to make sure the dogs were not on his heels.

The leg smelt something awful and was matted with blood and saliva and Gaston nearly threw up, but he reasoned that he was no different from the dogs. He was a scavenger. The meat could last a week — longer if he rationed it. He would live at least that long. He indulged in the banquet, burying his face in the torn limb. It was still warm. Gaston moaned and groaned as he ate, the blood running down his cheeks.

Old Jack was not that old at all, but it was what everyone called him — Old Jack. Even the blacks called him that. He didn't mind. There was little formality in the bush and even fewer social graces.

This boundary ride was tougher than usual and it would be at least two more days before they could get back home. There were many animals missing and many of the fences were broken, and they figured there were probably a hundred head or so running around in the wild. Some of the missing animals were found and mustered, and Jack put down those that were lame. Dingoes were taking a lot of the stock, running around in packs leaving carcasses in their wake. Jack didn't hesitate to shoot them if he could. To him they were good for nothing — 'bloody pests'.

On this hot, dry April day Jack was saddle-sore. He hoped that it hadn't gone. He reckoned that the shack was about an hour's ride away; that is, if it was still standing. Nobody had been there for a year and everyone knew that the wet was worse this year and the winds had been fierce.

'Johnno, Willie. We'll rest the horses at the hut and have a smoke for a while. Tell the others to meet us there.'

The hut was indeed still there. He had built it well. Before Jack could dismount, Willie had entered the hut. Jack got off the animal, took a stretch and then proceeded to remove the bridle and saddle.

'Boss, boss, come quick. Have a look at this. Look in the hut, there's something in there.'

Jack grabbed his rifle and followed Willie. Perhaps it was an animal — a dingo.

Jack thrust the old door aside. For a few moments he said nothing … He took it all in. There was graffiti, names, drawings and some kind of calendar. The stench was ripe. There were fruit cores and an animal bone. Whoever was living here had been here recently; there were footprints all over the place.

'Boss, look at this,' said Willie. It was a piece of bark with some form of writing scratched on it.

Jack took it outside into the sunlight. He tried to decipher the writing.

'It looks like … Help, Gast … US Arm … No, wait. It's US Army … A soldier has been here. An American. What in God's name is an American soldier doing in this place? … Willie, Strike-a-Light, Johnno, go ride and see if you can find anything else. Look around the place. Keep your eyes open for whitefella soldiers.'

It was just another day for the forgotten American. The search for food was not getting any easier. He did not know how much longer he could last. The resolve and the will to live had all but deserted him, and he really did not care any more. He was sure that he was going to die in this place, just like Arthur and the others. It seemed that nobody was looking anymore and nobody ever came to this part of the world. It was nearly noon, time to start back to the shack, although he had found nothing in the way of food. It was getting tougher to walk on the beach, but it was the quickest way back.

Gaston stopped and squinted his eyes. At first, he thought that the figure up ahead was a steer, but then he realised it looked like a horse, with a rider, about a hundred yards away. Gaston tried to call out but nothing happened. The man on the horse seemed to have heard his mute exclamation, because he looked in his direction and leaned forward on the saddle. He started towards Gaston, who was struck dumb and he could not move. He felt sure that if he looked again the figure would be gone. But it was still there, and getting closer. It was real. The rider was getting off the horse and was walking towards him. Gaston could hear some shouting, but couldn't make it out.

'You whitefella stay there. Don't go 'way — stay there. Are you a Jap? Or a whitefella? Don't move. Who are you? Where do you come from?'

Gaston could hear the voice but couldn't understand the language. It sounded like English, but strange. The speaker, a young Aboriginal man, kept talking as he walked towards Gaston. 'What's your name? What the bloody hell you doin' here?'

Soon the man was beside him. Grady wasn't frightened, just emotionally frozen. He thought that the black man looked like some sort of ranch hand.

'Ol' Jack is looking for you. You wanna ride Charley? You want to ride my horse?' Gaston could not speak. He could only shake his head.

'You come with me. I walk with you. Take you to Ol' Jack. He's looking for you. You look crook. My name's Strike-a-Light. Do you want a smoke?'

Jack was still examining the interior of the hut when somebody said that Strike-a-Light was returning and that there was someone with him.

Jack looked in the direction of the beach, his eyes squinting under the hot sun. Strike-a-Light was walking his horse towards the hut and there was a figure walking behind the horse. It was a man, dressed in what appeared to be rag clothes. Jack could see that he was in bad shape. His hair and long beard were bleached white by the sun. He walked in a crouched fashion, slowly and with a distinctive limp.

'This is a whitefella, but he says nothing,' said Strike-a-Light. 'He was walking along the beach; his eyes are dead.'

Jack walked towards the figure. 'Are you all right, mate? Are you an American? How long have you been here? Willie, get him some water.'

Gaston looked at Jack and reached out his hand. He tried to speak, but no words came out. His throat was dry and it had been eight weeks since he had spoken to anyone.

'Gaston, my name is Grady Gaston.' He spoke slowly. 'I'm a Staff Sergeant from the 321st Squadron. Our group is at Iron Range. Our bomber crashed in December. I'm the only one left. All the others are dead.'

Jack had heard about the crash, but had not conducted any search. It was not his business. Burketown was too far away.

'Jesus Christ, did you walk all this way? What are you doing in this part of the world? There's nothing here.'

'I guess we got lost,' said Grady. 'We thought that we were near Cairns.'

'You're a bloody long way from Cairns, mate. It's about five hundred miles to the south-east.'

Gaston drank eagerly from Jack's canteen. Water had become a prized acquisition. There was never enough and this was pure joy.

'Do you want something to eat?' asked Jack.

'Have you got any Luckys?'

'What was that?'

'Do you have any cigarettes?'

'I've got tobacco. I'll roll you one.'

Gaston took the cigarette and inhaled vigorously. The Capstan was a strong brand and Gaston coughed and dry retched. It had been so long, but he was not going to be denied.

'We don't have too much tucker, just some cold beef and some bread. It's a little stale, but it's okay.'

To Gaston it was a banquet. Nobody said anything while he ate.

Gaston began to tell Jack the story of the crash. He told him about Dale, about Dyer and Arthur.

'You blokes were dead-set unlucky,' said Jack. 'There's a fence line only about two miles from here. You could have found it and followed it back to Seven Emus. It's a wonder that none of my boys found you.'

Gaston could only shake his head. He continued his story, but the tale was interrupted by Willie who came running in with the news that they had found the remains of at least two bodies on the beach.

'It's John and Arthur,' said Gaston. 'They're my buddies. Leave them. Don't touch them.' Gaston tried to get up.

'It's okay, mate,' said Jack. 'Just take it easy. We'll take care of everything. It's too late to start back to my place now. We'll set off in the morning. I'll take you there and everything will be okay.'

Gaston ate too much and became bloated. Willie had mixed up some johnny cakes and Grady gorged himself until he threw up. It was good to feel bloated, and to have that rare feeling of not being hungry or thirsty.

He was more thankful than ever that he was still alive, but he wished that the others were all here with him. For the first time in weeks, Gaston believed that there was going to be a tomorrow. He did not sleep that night.

CHAPTER TEN

'His nerves were very bad'

YOUNG John Keighran could hear a commotion in the front paddock. The dogs were barking. He looked out of the window and saw riders coming through the front gate. It was his dad and the others. He ran out to meet them. Jennie was there too, with young Max. Jack waved and began to dismount. John could see that there was a strange figure riding Burketown. He was bouncing up and down on the saddle and had a firm grip on the saddle horn. Willie had the reins and was leading the horse up to the front of the house.

'Get some tucker ready and make up a bed,' said Jack. 'This is Grady. He's an American whose plane crashed near Burketown. We found him on the coast, near the old hut. He's going to be staying for a few days. We'll send word to Borroloola.'

The ride had been very hard on Gaston, but he didn't care. Jack led him to the porch and sat him in a large basket chair that was Jack's favourite chair. Many of the station hands and house servants had gathered to get a look at the strange visitor. They seldom saw any white men on the property and no one had even seen an American. With his bleached blond hair, long whiskers and torn clothes, his presence was compelling. There was much pushing and giggling when Gaston spoke in his thick Alabama drawl. When someone rolled him another smoke, Gaston told his story again. He recalled the crash and the aftermath.

'What was the name of the river where we lost Dale?' asked Gaston. 'Jack, what do you call it? The big river that runs into the sea?'

Jack told him that it was the Robinson, a dangerous and deadly river, particularly during the wet season. This was one thing that Gaston already knew.

In his official report of the incident Gaston recalled the events of the next few days:

Jack killed a young goat and even though I heard that goat meat was not very good, it sure tasted good to me. He fixed a good meal of it and gave me lots of milk. The next morning he killed a young bullock. I guess I ate too much too soon because I got very sick. At the time of the crash, I weighed 168 lbs, but now I was down to about 100 lbs.

During the sick spell, Jack was very good to me and in three or four days I was able to start getting around a little bit. My old tattered clothes were stiff as a board, but he took them off me and gave me some civilian clothes that were about two sizes too big. I stayed with him for two weeks, during which time I gradually began to pick up weight and feel as though I could go on again. He sent one of his boys to a police outpost located at a place called Borroloola, 75 miles away. It was the first case the police had handled in seven years. At the time, there were fifteen or twenty soldiers on patrol duty in that section. With the aid of the black boy as a guide, they blazed a trail through country where no vehicle had ever travelled and after two and one half days of hard work, they reached the place where I was.

They then went to the cabin I had used and picked up the bodies of Lt Dyer and Lt Speltz after which we went to the town of Borroloola. This was May 4. I stayed with the policeman for a day or two while he arranged to have a small aeroplane pick me up at a place called Anthony's Lagoon. The soldiers put me in their truck and drove 185 miles to a small field where the aeroplane would land. The plane arrived next day. We flew to a place called Camooweal where we spent the night and the next day he took me to Cloncurry. Everyone was so nice to me. I had intended to keep my long hair and beard until I could join some of my former friends, but the barber insisted that I let him cut it off which I did. The whole town was very good to me, giving me money, clothing and anything that I might need and taking me to their homes for meals.

Gaston's report was an exercise in brevity. The soldiers who came to the aid of the American were essentially members of the North Australia Observation Unit, commonly refereed to as Nackeroos. The unit was formed in May 1942 with Major W. E. H. Stanner, a noted anthropologist, the appointed commander.

The NAOU's duties were to patrol the northern coastal areas of Australia looking for any signs of the enemy. They also operated coastwatch stations and had an effective signals network for the Top End. The number of personnel, mostly expert horsemen, peaked at 550, including 59 Aboriginal workers, guides and labourers. Nackeroos were stationed around the coast at Normanton, Karumba, Inverleigh, Armraynad, Burketown and Borroloola. The main gap in their patrol areas was the 400-mile strip from Burketown to Borroloola. No one believed that this area posed any threat from invasion, particularly in the wet. The Nackeroos had been involved with the search for *Little Eva*'s crew since early December. Stan Chapman had driven Crosson and Wilson to Burketown after they had wandered into the Escott property.

Shortly after the body of Dale Grimes was discovered, the NAOU Platoon based at Borroloola had assisted Ted Heathcock with a new search. Lieutenant Romney Cole had dispatched a land patrol to search the area near the Wearyan River. Corporal Keith Ledingham had joined Ted Heathcock and two Aboriginals in a search by canoe in the areas near the MacArthur and Robinson rivers. The searches proved futile.

Weeks later, when word reached the NAOU at Borroloola that Gaston had been found, Corporal Ted Pattison, who was in charge at the time, immediately gathered together clothes, tobacco and toiletries and sent three Nackeroos in a flat-bed truck to Seven Emus. Pattison would never forget his first impression of Gaston as he climbed down from the truck on the afternoon of May 4th:

His hair and beard had gone completely white and his teeth were loose. He was more or less a walking skeleton. He came up to me and said, 'I believe you were responsible for sending me the clothes. One thing I want to thank you for was the toothbrush, it was just what I needed.' While he was in town, he stayed at the police station. The copper told me that Gaston was so hungry that he used to raid the kerosene refrigerator all night, going backwards and forwards to get little snacks.

Another Nackeroo, Barney Young, recalled:

He ate so much that he had a big bulbous belly, like a pregnant woman. He had such a sweet tooth that everything he ate had to have jam on it. Even the bully beef was covered in plum jam.

The Nackeroos, all experienced bushmen, marvelled at the resolve and resilience of the strange little man from Frisco City, Alabama. He was treated with awe and respect. No one in living memory had ever approached his feat of surviving 141 days alone in the Gulf country.

Barney Young never forgot his time spent with Gaston:

He'd kept a little bottle that contained four special survival matches. These had little blue heads on them and you could see how he'd worn down the top half off each match, trying to strike it. I asked him why he'd kept them and he replied, 'I'm taking these back to show the top brass how useless they are.' There was also a little tin that he'd used to keep some melon seeds in. These little melons grew wild up there, but they weren't worth eating as far as we were concerned. However, Grady reckoned they were the sweetest things he'd ever tasted and he wanted to take the seeds home to America to grow them.

When Gaston learned that the town had a telegram facility, he asked Nackeroo Jack Twyford to send a message to his mother, Wattie, in Alabama:

Dear Mother. Still alive and feeling good now. On way back to camp. Will write when get in and give details. Love Grady.

Gaston's activities after he left Borroloola are described in his report:

I had been in Cloncurry a couple of days when on May 11 some American officers stopped at the Hotel and asked for me. They gave me a bundle of clothing and told me that Capt. M. J. Foster of San Antonio, Texas, had sent them and made arrangements for their aeroplane to pick me up on its return trip the next day. That day and night seemed like a very long time to me but at noon the following day they returned for me. We took off from Cloncurry at 1.30 pm and arrived in Townsville at about 5.30 pm where Capt. Foster met me and brought me to the hospital where I am now slowly recovering. I have since seen my former pilot Lt Crosson who told me he and Sgt Loy Wilson, from Columbus, Ohio, had been picked up on December 18. I was very happy to know that at least some of our crew had been saved.

Gaston never knew the full impact of his arrival in Cloncurry. He had been in the town for only a few hours when he visited the local police station. Vince Peel was on the desk when Gaston confronted him:

'I was told by my superiors to report to this station. I'm Staff Sergeant Grady Steen Gaston, serial number 14013385, Wireless Operator of the Liberator Bomber which crashed at Moonlight Creek, near Burketown, on December 2nd, 1942.'

Peel took down the details of Gaston's ordeal for his report, which was completed on 17 May.

Galligan's reaction to Gaston not only being found but actually walking through the front door of his station can only be imagined. It was he who had called off the search in early February. He was mortified to learn that not only had Gaston survived but at the time of the search being aborted there were three Americans alive only a few days ride to the north-west of Hagarty's search party.

Vince Peel was still compiling his report when Galligan thought it prudent to attach his summation of the incident. He knew that Carroll would be asking the same questions and thinking the same thoughts — as would the American military. Galligan had called off the search while three Americans were still alive. Moreover, Hagarty was only a relatively short distance from the old shack and it was virtually certain that he would have stopped and searched the old hut.

Peel's report merely recounted the fact that Grady Gaston had walked into the station and told his story of the saga. It would be up to Galligan to cover his tracks. His report to Carroll, which was attached to Peel's, was cleverly worded but undoubtedly an attempt to vindicate his actions:

The original search for the lost aircraft and the crew began on December 18th.

The searchers numbered thirty-five, including Constables Marsh and Tracker Norman. From what I can gather there was no proper organisation or co-operation between them to effectively carry out the search. Many of the men had no knowledge of the country they were going into, and for various reasons the number was too unwieldy to be effective. Had Sergt. Nuss, Constables Hagarty and Marsh and their trackers formed a separate party they may have picked up the tracks of the four men missing and contacted the Mornington Island Aboriginals who picked up tracks on Rainbow Creek and on the beach. When word of the tracks having been found was received, it was impossible to get there from Burketown.

When Constables Hagarty and Marsh got into that country some weeks later, the rain that had fallen in the meantime had obliterated any traces of the tracks that existed earlier, and the missing men had travelled up to two hundred miles from where the bomber went down. From the information I received, I instructed Constable Hagarty to abandon the search.

The implication of Galligan's report is obvious: Nuss erred by not organising an effective search in the first instance. The Americans would not have died had they been found in late December. The fact that the Americans 'had travelled up to two hundred miles from where the bomber went down' suggests that no rational man could have expected such a heroic trek, or for the men to have survived for so long.

Galligan's most fundamental mistake was in calling off the search from Cloncurry while Hagarty was still at Wollogorang. He should have left the decision up to Hagarty, who was undoubtedly one of the most efficient and experienced bushmen in the Queensland Police Force. The Hagarty party were rested and had fresh supplies and mounts, and another week of searching would have mattered little in the allocation of police resources. It was Galligan's decision to reassign Hagarty to a routine matter in Lawn Hill that consigned John Dyer and Arthur Speltz to their fate in the savage wilderness of the Australian Gulf country.

After the abandonment of the search for the Americans, the men of the Queensland Police Force could have been forgiven for believing that they had seen the last of the Liberator of Moonlight Creek.

Harry Nuss quickly regained his pre-*Little Eva* insignificance. However, one day in May 1943, a boy from the Burketown Post Office delivered a letter to the station:

Headquarters
Unites States Army Service of Supply
Office of the Quartermaster
Base Section No 2

Subject: Location of Isolated Burial.

To: Sgt Nuss — Civilian Police (Queensland)

1. Information has been received at this office concerning an isolated burial of an American soldier, Charles B. Workman, a member of the 321st Bomb Squadron.

2. According to information received at this office you were a member of the burial party.

3. Disinterment of this burial is now contemplated and it is necessary that this office be furnished with all information regarding the location of this grave — a map or sketch if possible to guide the disinterment detail.

4. It would be greatly of help in locating this grave for disinterment.

For the Quartermaster.

M.A. Beyers,

Capt. Q.M.C.

Graves Reg. Officer.

Nuss was puzzled by the letter. Surely the Yanks knew that there were four bodies found near the wreck. And what sort of country did they think it was out there? He couldn't believe they wanted a road map to the plane — a map of the worst and most desolate country you could come across. Prudently, Nuss decided to respond through Galligan in Cloncurry. He directed Marsh to compile a response, which was dated 22 April 1943:

I have to report with reference to the above, that it is almost impossible to draw a sketch of the country passed through from here to the plane. There is an old road within 15 miles of the plane, but from there on it is all thick ti-tree scrub and in my opinion impossible to traverse that distance without clearing a road first. It is impossible to direct the party from here to the plane; the only means of locating it is for Tracker Norman and myself to accompany the party; there is only a pad to follow after leaving Gum Hole, and it would be quite easy to follow the wrong one.

R. J. Marsh
Constable No. 3764

Nuss soon forgot about the letter and he tried hard to forget the whole *Little Eva* saga. At best, his conduct and leadership during the ordeal was satisfactory; at worst, it was deemed ordinary and probably did nothing for his reputation or his career.

Just before noon on 4 July 1943, Nuss was alerted to the arrival of a group of soldiers from Iluka. One wore the uniform of the US Army and he was looking for Police Sergeant Harold Nuss.

The American introduced himself as Staff Sergeant Robert Joseph Dent, from the Office of the Quartermaster, United States Army, Base Section 2. He said that he had been ordered to retrieve the bodies of the four American airman killed in the crash of a United States aircraft the previous December, and that he had been authorised to recover the military inventory that was in Nuss's possession. He referred to the letter written by the graves registration officer, Captain Beyers, seeking directions to the crash area.

Nuss's response showed his frustration. 'It's not possible to direct you to the area. It's too isolated. It's in the middle of nowhere. You would just get lost yourself and then this whole bloody mess would start again.'

The Staff Sergeant's response was equally blunt. 'I have a copy of a letter from a Commissioner Carroll in Brisbane.'

Nuss read the letter. The past would die hard. Once again Nuss was the district incumbent.

Adverting to your suggestion that you be furnished with a sketch which would enable you to locate the place where the body of Charles B. Workman is buried. I am informed that it is almost impossible for the Police at Burketown to supply you with a sketch, which would be of any value, and would suggest that, whenever you decide to take action for disinterment, I will arrange for a member of the Police Force from Burketown to

accompany you. Might I suggest also that you communicate with Superin-
tendent Stretton, Northern Territory Police Force, Alice Springs, in relation
to the information which I have supplied you that concerns the human
remains taken to Borroloola Police Station, which are possibly those of 2nd
Lieutenant D. V. Grimes, a member of the crew of the ill-fated aircraft.

If you think I can be of any further assistance to you in this matter, please
communicate with me again.
Yours faithfully
C. J. Carroll
Commissioner of Police
Brisbane Qld

The Australian commander at Iluka was prepared to make available
two men, horses and pack animals for the trip, but Dent needed Nuss's
deputy, Marsh, and a tracker to lead the group to the area.

Dent stayed at Burketown while preparations were being made
for the journey. In conversations with Nuss he spoke about the significance of July 4th to the American people, and told him that the
American military spared no expense or effort in locating the
bodies or remains of lost servicemen. It did not matter where they
lay, they would be recovered and returned to their families or
reburied in military cemeteries; it was the least a grateful nation
could do.

At 2.00 pm on July 8th, Roy Marsh, Norman, Dent and Privates
Hutcheson and Hayden left Burketown for Durriejellpa. The plane
was located at 3.30 pm on July 11th. The remains of Workman,
McKeon, Hilton and Geydos were removed from their makeshift
graves and rolled onto blankets. It was an onerous task. The remains
were then strapped to the pack animals and the group returned to
Burketown, arriving on July 14th.

Nuss had prepared a list of the inventory that he had stored at the
rear of the station: five parachutes; three back rests, three complete sets
of harness and part of another, two life preservers, one leather jacket,

three revolvers (obsolete), portion of bombsight and one wristlet watch.

Dent signed for the equipment and the next day he returned to Townsville. Nuss hoped that this would be the end of the matter. Once again, he yearned for anonymity, the ordinary and the mundane.

When Gaston eventually returned to the United States he found himself a military hero. The shy, withdrawn and introverted farmer from Alabama became a reluctant celebrity. The nation's newspapers showed little restraint. The headlines portrayed a new national hero: 'Lone Yank Survives 141 Day Trek in Australian Wilds — Airman Lost Five Months In Jungle'.

The Los Angeles *Examiner* had the following account:

Survivor of US Bomber Crew Eats Raw Fish — fights wild dogs for food

One of the most amazing 'escape' stories of the war was unfolded today by Staff Sergeant Grady Gaston of Frisco City Alabama.

There have been numerous instances of airmen who have made forced landings in the jungles and spent weeks beating their way back to civilisation, but Gaston's story tops them all.

For five incredible months, he wandered over a barren peninsula at the northern tip of Australia, living on uncooked snakes, fish, beef, and whatever else he could get. He had no means of starting a fire, and for days on end he went without food and water.

Gaston fought off starvation with meat ripped from the carcass of a dead calf that had been half-eaten by wild dogs until finally on March 21 a native found him and led him to a white cattle rancher.

The sensational account had more errors than just Gaston's rescue date, but it hardly mattered. A ready-made hero was being thrust on the American public. Other newspapers resorted to dramatic and lurid storytelling. Only one newspaper, *The Saskatchewan Star*

Phoenix, conveyed any sense of the tragedy of those who had perished. The headline of 30 August 1943 was succinct: 'One Came Back'.

The same newspaper also revealed that 'Gaston has since made a rapid recovery. He has gained nearly sixty pounds and looks fairly fit. But in his tired, strained eyes there is the faraway look of a man who has walked with death in dark places.'

Gaston was also a frequent guest on various network radio programs. In July 1943, he participated in a radio program spotlighting lost aircraft and newly found national heroes. Amid engine noises and battle sound effects, an NBC announcer addressed the American public:

'Day after day, we read those words "missing in action". We wonder what was the fate of the boys who manned those ships — where they are now — will they return? Sometimes months later they pop up again, back in civilisation, back to their buddies and families who had almost given up hope. We the people have not heard of a more desperate fight against slow death than that put up by Staff Sergeant Grady S. Gaston of Frisco City Alabama. He's home on furlough now. Sergeant Gaston, welcome home and welcome to the microphone.'

'Thank you, Mr Boulton. It's good to be home.'

'Tell me, Sergeant, what was it you thought most about during all those weeks by yourself?'

Responding to questions, Gaston recounted the ordeal from a censored script.

'Well, Mr Boulton, during the day I spent as much time as my strength would allow looking for food and night after night I would dream of home in Alabama when the crepe myrtle was in bloom; of walking down a shady street to the drugstore, then I would wake up and see the desolate Australian wasteland; the glistening hot dry sand.'

'What now, Sergeant?'

'I'm in tiptop shape now and report for duty July 29th. I'm ready and anxious to go back.'

Grady Gaston was neither ready nor anxious to return to duty. From his new posting in Salt Lake City, he wrote the hardest letter of his life:

Dear Miss Speltz,

I am Sergeant Gaston, a crew member that was on the plane that your brother Lt Speltz was on. I don't know how to write this but if I say anything that I shouldn't, please forgive me.

The authorities have probably told your Mother the details that I told them. I also gave them Lt Speltz' wallet and watch and the money he had on him. I hope she got it okay.

As you probably already know Lt Speltz passed away in his sleep Feb. 24th while I was lying by his side. It was just about more than I could stand, for this left me alone and it was almost two months later that I was found by a native and finally got out to civilisation to the hospital on May 12th.

I have been home on leave and have reported back for duty now. I am in Salt Lake City and will leave before Sunday, don't know just where I will go from here, but I don't think I will be any good for anything else, for I can't seem to get over the past, it just keeps pressing on my mind at all times.

Lt Speltz was a good man. He was a hero and he was my buddy. I don't now how to express my feelings towards his family, but if there is any way I can help clear up things in your mind, don't fail to let me hear from you.

Sincerely a friend.

S/Sgt. Grady S. Gaston

Prov. Sqdn A

Army Air Base

Salt Lake City, Utah.

Gaston's next posting was in Casper City, Wyoming. He was

attached to the 461st Squadron in a training capacity. While in Casper, Gaston met a young woman called Naomi. She was living near the base with her sister and her sister's husband:

My brother-in-law was based at the Casper Air Base and brought Grady home one night. I met him again later. I was a 'Rosie the Riveter' type and worked from 11 pm to 7 am. He was standing, as were all workers and soldiers. It was the last bus of the night and we sat together. It was a cold night — below zero. He was very quiet, but he seemed anxious. His nerves were very bad. We met again in a non-cons club in 1944. Casper Base closed in early 1945. Grady was transferred to the Kirkland Air Base in Albuquerque. I went home to my parents in Kansas. He got a cross-country flight and proposed in Salina, Kansas. We were married on March 31st 1945.

The other two survivors of the *Little Eva* ordeal found themselves more capable of social and military involvement. Norm Crosson was allowed some rest and recreation in Sydney. On 12 January 1943, he wrote a letter to his parents, Margaret and John Crosson of Dryden, Cincinnati. It was the first time they had heard any details of the tragedy. After recalling the essentials of the mission and his rescue, Crosson wrote:

I am now in one of the big cities and will have a two-week rest. I am feeling fine now and soon will be OK. I am a little nervous now when flying but should get over it soon. Our squadron censoring officer said it would be okay to send this. I hope the main office does not stop it. If I do not get over my jitters, I will probably get sent back to the States. I could have asked to be sent back when I got in, but did not want to. I had better start out and get something to eat. It is great to be able to get ham and eggs, cokes and hamburgers and all those things we have been missing.

Crosson eventually returned to Iron Range and the 90th Bomb Group. In February he was transferred to New Guinea. Loy Wilson also served in New Guinea. He returned to the United States and became an instructor in the Field Training Branch. On 17 April 1943, he was awarded the Purple Heart.

Harry Nuss never again had to encounter anything approaching the significance of the *Little Eva* incident. The remainder of his career in the Queensland Police Force was uneventful — just the way he wanted it. His last posting was in the country town of Toowoomba. Harry Nuss retired in 1964, and would die before the end of the decade.

Roy Marsh left the Queensland Police Force in 1950. He vanished from the outback and from public record.

Bob Hagarty left Gregory Downs in 1950 and served in other rural centres until his retirement in Cooktown in 1969. The Liberator of Moonlight Creek never left him. Until the day he died, Hagarty told anyone who would listen, 'I would have found them; just a couple more days and I would have found them.' He now rests with his wife Alice in a small plot in the Cooktown cemetery. The inscription on his tombstone reads:

Robert Phillip Hagarty.
6–7–1909 — 14–9–1991.
A Police Officer of Channel, Gulf, Cape Country and Cooktown.
An Accomplished Bushman and Horseman.

The wounds that Ted Heathcock suffered during the First World War finally claimed him during the Second. He died some time in 1943, a much admired man.

Old Jack Keighran always regretted selling Seven Emus in 1948. He reckoned that he should have sold it a few years later, when both property and cattle prices were better. He bought a much smaller property, a few miles from Seven Emus, called Greenbank, and spent the rest of his days doing what he had always done — minding cattle and minding his business. He died in 1974 and his boys buried him in the back paddock, which is what Jack would have wanted.

In July 1980 a reporter for the *Greenville News* decided to explore the myth and legend of the person 'Little Eva'. It was revealed that 'Eva' was in fact Genevieve Davis Coyle, who had spent her entire life in Greenville. It is believed that she died in 1960. Her daughter, Jacquelynne, confirmed that Eva was a no-nonsense woman, who had once thrown a man through a glass door and *was* around 350 pounds. Eva's husband, Jack, survived her and remembered Eva's place as being 'Nice — she was good to the boys. There was always some jitterbug-ging and the beer was always cold'. But he reckoned that Eva was more like 250 pounds than 350. Eva/Genevieve, unaware of her place in history, rests in the Beaver Dam Baptist Church on Route 1, Pelzer.

Norm Crosson and Loy Wilson returned to the United States and enjoyed successful careers in the American military and in commerce. Crosson died at his home in Simpsonville, South Carolina, in May 1989.

Loy Wilson died in the arms of his beloved Billie, on 13 July 1991. They had been married for fifty years.

Gaston returned to live in Frisco City, Alabama, in a house 400 metres from where he was born. In 1946 he became the father of a daughter called Mary-Lou. There was further tragedy in his life when the young girl was diagnosed as suffering from cerebral palsy. Gaston did not continue his career in the military. For forty years he delivered mail in the Frisco City area. It seems that he never recovered from his ordeal in the Australian outback and he would seldom recount the incident. Naomi Gaston recently revealed that the only time Grady would confront the *Little Eva* demons was 'when he was imbibing. His nerves were very bad'.

In 1977, Gaston told researcher Jim Eames:

We didn't give survival all that much thought. We thought that we would be picked up in a matter of hours. We didn't realise, of course, that we were

hundreds of miles from where we should have been. When we did move off,
we just happened to go the wrong way. Water was always the problem and
there wasn't that much eatin' goin' on. The others were city people. They
wouldn't eat snakes and the like. I was born and raised in Frisco City, with
a population of about 2000 people. I would chew anything, 'cause it was
the only way to stay alive.

In 1984, in response to a question about the incident, he was succinct: 'It was 141 days of hell'.

It was one of the very few letters Gaston wrote. In 1985 he expressed little interest in a proposed screen treatment of the saga. He had even less interest in the annual 90th Bomb Group veterans reunions.

Gaston fought both his demons and leukaemia in the last years of his life. The chemotherapy treatment for the disease tortured his wasted body. He eventually lost a third of his body weight. It was similar to his plight in 1943, but in the mid-1990s his body lacked the capacity to resist and his mind lacked the resolve.

The *Little Eva* demons came back to haunt Gaston one more time. On 19 December 1995, Wiley Woods Jr, the 90th Bomb Group's official historian, received a letter from Sergeant First Class Drew T. Holliday, from the American Embassy in Canberra, Australia.

Dear Mr Woods,
To be brief, I was recently approached by an Australian citizen who has in
his possession a shell inscribed with a message concerning the December
1942 crash of tail 123762, 'Little Eva', Staff Sergeant Gaston's B-24
Liberator bomber.
  The man now in possession of the shell apparently wants to sell it, and
has been looking for various buyers, among them the United States.

Frankly, it seems terribly incongruous to demand money for such an artefact of human tragedy.

For that reason, I have begun work with the Australian War Memorial, one of Australia's most respected historical institutions, to attempt to have the shell donated to their museum as a lasting and poignant symbol of the human sacrifices and bonds between America and Australia. The War Memorial agrees with this viewpoint. If we can convince the current owner to donate it, they would place the shell on permanent display in their museum here in Australia's capital.

However, before we can attempt to persuade the owner to donate the shell, we must verify its authenticity to the greatest extent possible. Staff Sergeant Gaston is literally the only person on earth who can do that.

If possible, would you please pass this letter on to Staff Sergeant Gaston, with our request to confirm whether he did, indeed, leave a message scratched on a shell.

Also, what are his personal sentiments, if any, regarding the shell? What does he think of the idea to have it placed in an area of honour in the National War Memorial Museum?

Mr Woods, this is a matter of great interest and potential importance to a great many people. We very much appreciate your help with the case.
Sincerely,
Drew T. Holliday
Sergeant First Class
United States Army

Wiley Woods had long been a stalwart for the 90th Bomb Group. He was also a protector of their history and heritage. He had spent years writing the official history of the group. It was called *Legacy of the 90th Bombardment Group — The Jolly Rogers* and was hailed as being one of the best of its type. His archives, notes and records have been meticulously catalogued and stored in various institutions. He had never ceased in his search for data on his beloved organisation, and was one of the few veterans who possessed the enthusiasm to send and receive copious letters on the men, machines and exploits of the 90th. Unlike many of his fellow veterans, age had not wearied him. With the exception of a minor hearing problem, Woods — then in his late seventies — was as good as new.

The letter from Canberra came as a surprise. He was well versed with in *Little Eva* saga and his account of the tragedy in his book was masterly in its narrative, brevity and authenticity.

Drew Holliday had chosen his contact well, even more than he knew. By the mid–1990s, Wiley Woods was a one of the few people who could claim to be both friend and confidant of Grady Gaston.

January 4, 1996.
Dear Sgt. Holliday,
I referred your letter of December 19, 1995 to Grady Gaston in Frisco City, Alabama, for a reply.

I have just talked to Grady by phone. He asked that I advise you that he cannot remember if he left a shell with a message on it. He said it is possible that he could have left such a message, but cannot recall if he did.

Grady is suffering from leukaemia and has lost 50 pounds. He said that he is not up to writing and ask that I reply for him. If you learn more information about the shell that may aid Grady in recalling it please let me know and I will pass it on to Grady.

It would be a nice addition to the War Memorial if the shell could be authenticated.

It is a shame that Grady's health is so bad. He is a major part of the history of the 90th Bomb Group.
Sincerely yours
Wiley O. Woods Jr

The man who claimed ownership of the shell was Harry Mackney, from Mareeba in North Queensland. This was the same small town that served as a base for the squadrons of the 90th Bomb Group in 1942.

In a response to inquiries by Drew Holliday, Mackney gave an account of how the shell came into his possession:

The shell was given to me by my stepson in 1963. He had carried it around in his haversack for a number of years prior to that. He is now deceased. He said that he found the shell near a campfire in the McArthur river area of the Northern Territory.

Intrigued by the writing on the shell, he made some local enquiries. He was told that the shell could have something to do with a plane crash during the war. If authentic, it would be one that was originally picked up by an Aboriginal stockman and given to his boss — the head stockman — or manager — on that cattle station. It had subsequently been lost, or probably just dumped or forgotten.

My stepson carried it around for years in his haversack, which served to cut off a lot of the writing. However, I feel that enough remains to allow Mr Gaston to recognise his own hand.

Halliday sent a number of photographs of the item, which revealed some legible text:

'US Army B24. Bailed out Dec 4, 1942 Reached here Dec 24 1942'. There were four names scratched on the surface which were still legible: 'Grimes', 'Dyer', 'Speltz' and 'Gaston'. There was also some more text, but it was indecipherable after all these years.

The letter and photographs were sent to Gaston by Woods. In a subsequent letter to Holliday, Woods made an interesting comment:

From my conversation with Grady, I get the impression that Grady does not want the shell to be authentic.

Holliday was not be deterred. Interest in the artefact was

considerable. He wrote to Woods on 8 February 1996. The letter was virtually a plea:

> *If authenticated, the shell's formal and fitting entry into Australia's histor-*
> *ical heritage would be an event of some importance. The War Memorial has*
> *told me that this would have Ministerial involvement, press and television*
> *coverage, and possibly even involve the attention of the Prime Minister.*
> *Seven men died in this tragedy. Seven American families were left grieving.*
> *We could now give their deaths meaning.*

The response from Woods seemed to be the last word. After telling Holliday that he himself 'believed the shell to be authentic', he concluded:

> *I only wish that Grady could authenticate the shell and I am sorry that pos-*
> *itive identification will never occur. I feel that I am unable to be of further*
> *help on this puzzle, but I would appreciate your advising me of the final*
> *decision as to its authenticity.*

There is no question that the artefact was authentic. Gaston himself inadvertently confirmed its legitimacy. His official report on the incident, written shortly after his rescue, mentioned that the date of the bailout was December 4th. It was an error. The actual date was December 2nd. The date scratched on the shell was December 4th. Any potential forger would almost certainly have used the date revealed in numerous reliable accounts — December 2nd.

However, the opportunity to commemorate the men involved in the *Little Eva* saga was lost. The shell remained in Mareeba.

The world has changed since those dark days sixty years ago. The protagonists in the saga are long gone. The old shack that became the final home for the lost Americans has also disappeared. The only tangible reminder of this tragic event is the Liberator of Moonlight Creek.

Little Eva still lies in the same spot that proved so elusive sixty years ago. Although it is listed as a tourist attraction, few people visit the wreck. Norman Crosson could not have picked a more distant and isolated location to crash his aircraft.

However, over the years, *Little Eva* has been violated. The weapons and ordnance are long since gone and during the Sixties the four Pratt and Whitney engines were torn from the wing housings, presumably for use on other aircraft. The fuselage was broken up in the process and the wreck now bears little resemblance to its former glory. The few who now visit the wreck seem obliged to leave the legacy of graffiti on what remains of *Eva*'s superstructure. Despite its condition the wreck still radiates a feeling of intimidation and a doomed sense of history.

The story of the tragedy is now also part of historic folklore. There seems to be more myth than reality. The search for the truth has been as elusive as the original survivors were.

It would never occur to Grady Gaston, or any other of the Americans involved in this incident, that the odyssey has inspired generations of Aboriginal people to celebrate the event in a ritual dance called the Ka-Wayawayama — the Aeroplane Dance.

Indigenous people from north-west Queensland recreate the incident with much enthusiasm and vigour. The dance was originally created by an Aboriginal elder called Karrijiji (aka Frank) from the Yanyuwa people. Frank was involved in the original search for the men. Aboriginal people from the Yanyuwa and tribes who perform the ritual have transformed the *Little Eva* incident into Aboriginal folklore.

On 9 June 2001, the Aeroplane Dance was performed as part of the Warrawulla Festival at Borroloola. Surviving Aboriginal searchers were presented with Territory Defender Certificates by Lieutenant-General Peter Cosgrove.

John Keighran was also a recipient. He dedicated his certificate to his father, Old Jack, who had found Gaston all those years before. Strike-a-Light's son, Kelly Martin — Burrulangii — was there to receive the certificate for his late father. It was a big day for Borroloola and for the Aboriginal people.

In April 2003, a memorial was unveiled in the town of Doomadgee. The names of the ten crew-members of *Little Eva* are inscribed on a plaque. This Anzac Day event was one of the most important ever associated with the town. Representatives from the Queensland Police Force, the United States Military, the Australian Armed forces, Borroloola police, the Aboriginal people and local homesteaders attended the service.

This grouping was a representation of the protagonists involved in the original search, sixty years before.

The saga of *Little Eva* was a little-known incident in a conflict that was dealing with death every day. During the war, most American servicemen had seen the civilised Australia, but only a few like Gaston and his colleagues had experienced the savagery and isolation of this sparsely populated land.

Grady Gaston may have survived the ordeal, but he did not survive the experience.

On 8 January 1998, the Savage Wilderness claimed its final victim.

Sources

The Crash of Little Eva was researched and compiled from the original Queensland Police files at the Queensland State Archives in Brisbane. The numerous relevant reports and documents are filed under 'Air Crashes'. Much information — including service records, photographs and rare police documents — was supplied by the Queensland Police Museum.

Details about the American servicemen involved come from Grady Gaston's original official report, which has been in circulation among historians for decades. Less available and equally indispensable is the report by Lieutenant Norman Crosson, which I was able to locate.

Oral history research consisted of many verbal accounts and recollections from police and from 90th Bomb Group veterans as well as their surviving family members. My research also unearthed numerous letters, unpublished memoirs and other contemporary documents relating to the *Little Eva* story.

The following books were among the most useful:

Alcorn, John S. *The Jolly Rogers: History of The 90th Bomb Group During World War Two.* Historical Aviation Album, 1981.

Bailey, Ronald H. *The Home Front: U.S.A.* Alexandria, Virginia: Time Life Books, 1978.

Campbell, Christy. *The World War II Fact Book, 1939–1945.* London: Macdonald and Co, 1985.

Dennis, Peter with Jeffrey, Ewan Morris and Robin Prior. *The Oxford Companion to Australian Military History.* Melbourne: Oxford University Press, 1995.

Duwell, Martin and Dixon, R. M. W., eds, *Little Eva at Moonlight Creek and other Aboriginal Song Poems.* St Lucia: University of Queensland Press, 1994.

Eames, Jim. *The Searchers.* St Lucia: University of Queensland Press, 1999.

Gillison, Douglas. *Royal Australian Air Force. 1939–1942*, Canberra: Australian War Memorial, 1962.

Goralski, Robert. *World War II Almanac, 1931–1945: A Political and Military Record.* New York: Bonanza Books, 1981.

Green, William. *Famous Bombers of the Second World War.* London: Macdonald and Janes, 1977.

Hasluck, Paul. *The Government and the People 1942–1945.* Canberra: Australian War Memorial, 1970.

Jane's Fighting Aircraft Of World War Two: Bracken Books, 1989.

Johnstone, W. Ross. The Long Blue Line: Brisbane: Boolarong Publications, 1992.

Kennett, Lee. *For The Duration. The US Goes to War,* New York: Charles Scribner's & Sons, 1985.

Marks, Roger R. *Queensland Airfields, 50 Years On.* Brisbane: R&J Marks, 1994.

Martinez, Mario. *Lady's Men.* London: Leo Cooper, 1995.

Moore, John Hammond. *Over Sexed, Over Paid and Over Here.* St. Lucia: University of Queensland Press, 1981.

Perret, Geoffrey. *Old Soldiers Never Die.* New York: Random House, 1996.

Perret, Geoffrey. *Winged Victory – The Army Air Forces in World War II.* New York, Random House, 1993.

Walker, Richard. *Curtin's Cowboys.* Sydney. London: Harper Collins Publishers, 1986.

Wheal, Elizabeth Anne, Pope, Stephen and Taylor, James, *Encyclopaedia of the Second World War.* New Jersey: Castle Books, 1989.

Woods, Wiley O. *Legacy of the 90th Bombardment Group: The Jolly Rogers.* Turner Publishing Company, 1997.

Index